Touche

C000143500

Trevor Dean C.F.C.

Touched by God

The Story of Olive Allerton

Fount

An Imprint of HarperCollinsPublishers

To the Christian Brothers
whose support and active encouragement
have made it possible
for Olive's story to be told

First published in Great Britain in 1991 by Fount Paperbacks

Fount Paperbacks is an imprint of
HarperCollins Religious Division,
Part of the HarperCollins Publishing Group
77–85 Fulham Palace Road, London W6 8JB

Copyright © 1991 by Trevor Dean

Printed and bound in Great Britain by Cox & Wyman Ltd, Reading

Contents

1

In the steps of Mother Teresa

The 747 touched down, ran along the tarmac and then shuddered momentarily as the jets were put into reverse. Two minutes later the plane came to a halt, there was a flurry of activity as passengers opened up the overhead lockers and retrieved their hand luggage. The experienced ones hurried off to get as close to the top of the queue as they could, for they knew that four hundred passengers being processed through passport control at Calcutta could take anything up to an hour.

Olive did not worry about such things. She just waited in her seat until the hostess came long, handed her the aluminium crutches so that she could hoist herself to her feet, and hobbled to the hatch. Here she was settled into a wheel chair, rolled on to the mobile hoist and seconds later was being wheeled into the terminal. Passport control, baggage collection and customs took just over half an hour – Olive went through quickly thanks to the help from the hostess – and all that remained was to change some money. Five minutes later, with enough rupees in her bag to keep her going for two or three weeks, she settled down into the back seat of the taxi and said to the driver, "Mother Teresa's Home, Lower Circular Road".

At 11.00 p.m. Olive could not make out too much as they drove into the city, but she was conscious of a good deal of activity even at that hour. She was conscious too of a

1

growing sense of discomfort and nausea – the fish served on the plane had not agreed with her – and the closer she got to Mother Teresa's Home, the worse she felt. Ten minutes before she arrived she knew that she could go no further. She stopped the taxi, got out and was sick in the gutter. People appeared from nowhere, solicitous for the lady on crutches vomiting her heart out within an hour of reaching India. Complete strangers to Olive, they extended to her the warmth and friendliness she was to experience so often in the years to come. They cleaned up the mess, helped her back into the car, and on she sped as the taxi threaded its way to Circular Road.

Luckily this taxi driver was able to get directions as to where Mother Teresa's Home was, because finding one's own way there is not so easy. Along Chandra Bose Road, past Shishu Bhavan, and a right turn took her a hundred yards or so down Circular Road, and there it was. Nothing prepossessing – just a door in a wall with a notice above: "Missionaries of Charity". A ring on the bell and a few minutes later Olive was speaking to two of the Missionaries of Charity, the first of many Sisters with whom she was to be in contact. Volunteers come from all over the world to help Mother Teresa, but not too many of them arrive at midnight. Still, Olive was there on the doorstep, so the Sisters told her of a hostel nearby. They had the car brought out and went with her the short distance involved and arranged for her to say there. The place was very shabby by Australian or Western standards. "It was not dirty, but then again, it was not particularly clean", was Olive's comment. A bed, a table and a chair were the only furniture, but it was adequate, so Olive got into bed without delay. She was rather weary after the trip from Toowoomba to Brisbane in a light six-seater plane, and then the flight in the jumbo to Singapore and Calcutta.

Sleep did not come easily though, and her thoughts wandered back to Australia. Today was Tuesday, or rather Wednesday, seeing that it was now after midnight. With any luck the letters she had posted to Jean and Bill on the way to the airport would reach them before the weekend. Jean would probably get hers in Adelaide a day before Bill received his in Rydal near Lithgow in New South Wales. And how would they take it? Would they be annoyed that she had settled all her affairs and flown off to Calcutta without letting them know? Still, it was the only thing to do. They would have tried to stop her if they had known beforehand, but now they would soon get accustomed to the idea, shrug their shoulders and say, "Oh well, that's Mum!" Both Jean and Bill had their own families to think of, and with teenage daughters to look after they would not be too worried about Mum — after all, she had managed quite well in many situations in the past. This new venture with Mother Teresa was simply another incident in that pattern of unpredictable behaviour that made up her life.

The next morning Olive was up early so as to get to Mass at 6.45 at St Thomas's, two hundred yards down the road. There was no one in the office when she went along to arrange for a taxi. A lady was washing the floor, and Olive told her what she wanted, but there were no taxis to be had. There were rickshaws though, and Olive settled on one of these. Calcutta is the only place in India where rickshaws pulled by men are still allowed. Everywhere else they have been banned, but in Calcutta the rickshaw wallahs ply their trade to this very day, as Dominique Lapierre so vividly describes in *City of Joy*. For one human being to get into the shafts of a rickshaw and pull another human being along may seem demeaning, and it *is*. But when you have several thousand men in Calcutta depending on this for a livelihood, do you stand on principle, choose not to use a rickshaw, and so leave the wallah without a fare? Whether Olive thought of these things or rationalized the situation we do not know, but we do know that she booked this same man to pick her up each morning at the same time for the next week. That eventually stretched into a month, which is the period she remained in that particular hostel.

St Thomas's was a large school with a convent upstairs, and in the chapel here Olive found about thirty people gathered for the Eucharist. Olive was lucky to happen upon a building that had a lift in it, for that saved labouring up the stairs one at a time.

Back to the hostel for breakfast and into a taxi again, this time bound for Nirmal Hriday, the Home for the Dying. Nirmal Hriday means "Pure Heart" and was given to Mother Teresa after she appealed to the Government that something should be done for the destitute people who were dying every day at Howrah Station and in the streets of Calcutta.

Nirmal Hriday is right next to the Temple of Kali, the spouse of the Hindu god Shiva. In fact, what is now the Home for the Dying was once a hostel for pilgrims travelling to Calcutta to carry out their devotions to Kali, before it was handed over to Mother Teresa. A fifteen-minute drive brought Olive to Kaligat, the suburb in which the temple complex is located.

The streets all around are alive with vendors of flowers, garlands and fruit which may be taken as an offering to Kali. Nirmal Hriday is on one corner of the complex, with an open area immediately in front where the ambulance can pull in with stretcher cases. Olive's taxi took her right to the door and in no time she was inside. The men's ward opened out immediately before her, the floor being on two levels, with low beds on each level, two rows running along each wall with a corridor between. About forty men are usually accommodated in this large open area, and nearby is the Nurse's station from which Sister Luke, the nun in charge, keeps an eye on things. The women's ward is on the other side.

Olive introduced herself to Sister Luke, told her she had come to help, and asked if there was anything she could do. Sister Luke spoke to her for some minutes, but obviously she was sceptical – what could this old lady on crutches do? In fact, could she do anything worthwhile or would she be more hindrance than help?

With eighty dying people on your hands there is always something to be done, so Sister Luke excused herself to attend to some pressing task and Olive was left sitting there. After a time she realized that Sister Luke was really testing her out – would she find something she could do? At Nirmal Hriday the volunteers are expected to show some initiative. There is a host of things they can do, and directions as to what to do and how to do basic tasks are willingly given. But incidental jobs crop up and one can assist by coming forward and doing these.

While Olive was sitting there a boy came through the main door, past Olive and into the kitchen area. Olive took her cue, followed him into the kitchen, and asked if there was anything to do.

"No, not really. We've just finished the vegetables."

"Well, what about those fish? Do they have to be cleaned?"

"Yes, I suppose they do."

And with that Olive was on her way. She donned the apron she had brought with her, took out a kitchen knife she "just happened" to be carrying, and set to. She had just about finished scaling and cleaning the fish when one of the Sisters came in and asked, "Can anyone give Johnny a bath?" No answer was forthcoming, as everyone was occupied, so

5

after a brief pause Olive chimed in, "Yes, I should be able to do that."

When she got to Johnny it was not all that easy. He was twelve years old and suffering from St Vitus's Dance. As a result, arms were flailing about from time to time, and Olive had quite a job supporting herself with one of her crutches, washing Johnny in the bath and trying to restrain him from hitting things or people, herself included. However, she did manage, and once the job was done people realized that Olive was genuine in her offer to help, and she was accepted by the staff.

The next task was the distribution of pills and medications to the patients. The nurse in charge has a list which gives the diagnosis of each patient and what has been prescribed. For half an hour to an hour volunteers assist the regular staff – a patient might have difficulty getting a pill down, and a minute or so will be spent helping with this. Wounds or open sores will need dressing, a TB patient may be having difficulty breathing. Someone might need just the sense that there are other human beings about who care – sitting on a bed holding a hand, kneeling down and helping a person swallow some medicine – simple things, but precisely what a number of these dying people had previously been denied.

About 11 o'clock each morning rice is distributed on the front steps, and people from the neighbourhood gather with their metal containers, plates or makeshift receptacles. Then milk and biscuits are distributed to the children. Very young babies in arms are brought along by their mothers, children who are able to come by themselves from the age of three to ten or eleven receive a pannikin full, and if any milk is left over the old ladies who have been waiting patiently for this moment might score a cupful. But this happens only if the supply holds out.

Next comes the midday meal for the patients, with rice the basic ingredient, but depending on the day there is fish or meat, dahl and curry, possibly followed up with something sweet. It is pitiful to see a few patients who for the first time in their lives can eat as much as they want, and they call for a second, third and even a fourth helping of rice. If they are there long enough they come to realize that there will be food available tomorrow, and the next day, and the day after, and that there is no need to take in huge quantities each time it is available.

Normally, the volunteers work through the morning. Most of the work is finished by lunchtime, with just routine care necessary through the afternoon and night. Those patients who die are wrapped in a white shroud and laid in the mortuary, until taken off in the ambulance which does duty for all sorts of functions!

It would be hard to imagine sacks of coal being delivered in an ambulance in this country, but resources in India are infinitely less than in the West and this is particularly true of Calcutta. So when the same vehicle is pressed into service for all sorts of jobs in Calcutta you are simply grateful that the vehicle is available. Coal is needed to stoke the boilers, and is delivered regularly to Nirmal Hriday. This is one job that Olive could not do, and strong male volunteers would take the sacks of coal up to the flat-topped roof where the coal scuttle is situated.

Another regular job that Olive had to leave to others was the disinfecting of blankets. Each day, blankets used by patients would be soaked in a big vat filled with disinfectant. These would be wrung out, carried upstairs and hung out on the lines on the top of the flat-roofed building. That was a heavy task and required more strength than Olive could muster, and more agility than she had.

Even so, there were plenty of things for Olive to do and she was content and happy. She was not just "rusting away" as she had been afraid would have been her fate if she had remained at Symesthorpe in Toowoomba. Here she was with people who were on the verge of going to meet their Creator, and she considered it a privilege to be able to ease their last days and weeks on earth. She had begun what was – paradoxically – to be the most fruitful period of a full and crowded life. Who was this woman who flew into Calcutta to follow in the steps of Mother Teresa at the age of seventy-seven? What kind of person was she to leave the comforts of a rest home in Australia, where attention was danced upon her twenty-four hours a day, to turn around and put herself out to serve others in one of the most challenging – and for some people, one of the most depressing – cities in the world?

2

Childhood and youth at Worthing

Olive came into the world on 5th September 1904. Her father, William Kaye Edden, had very good connections in the English aristocracy, while his brother Harold moved in royal circles. He himself had been a boarder at Clifton, a big public school near Bristol, and had then gone into the army as a captain. He was a very good athlete, keen on hunting, shooting and fishing. He inherited eighty thousand pounds in the middle of the nineteenth century, and was one of the most eligible bachelors of his day. When he married he settled at Portsmouth and his wife bore him eight children. Then disaster struck the family.

William moved to Worthing, and there he began a new life and a new family with Olive's mother, who had been Ethel Fricker. Worthing is on the south coast of England and it was there that the two children were born, first Olive and fifteen months later John.

Ethel's family had migrated from Germany in the previous century, at a time of religious persecution, and the Frickers had lost a good deal of money. Ethel, who was quietly vivacious, had two sisters, and they were known as "The Three Graces". She had a beautiful figure, was very slim, with an 18-inch waist, and carried herself well. Olive's father used to say to her, "If your mother wore rags, you'd still know she was a lady." However, she did not have to wear rags! She would send up to Ravel or Worth in London, ordering a dress for a particular occasion, and never went into a shop to buy one. The dress would be sent direct to Shelley Lodge and never cost less than a thousand pounds. She never had to work and she was a lady of leisure.

William Edden was an astute businessman and built his fortune up to one and a half million pounds by the time of his death in 1917. The family had two houses in Worthing, and there were a number of domestic and ground staff to maintain them: two cooks, a butler, a kitchen maid, a parlourmaid, a housemaid and a nurse. When the family lived in Portsmouth, before Olive's birth, they had twenty horses, but the move to Worthing brought the number down to five because there just was not the room to keep them there. They did have a small piece of land next to their home, Shelley Lodge, but nowhere near big enough for twenty horses.

Olive was brought up in the saddle, and from an early age had her own horse. Her father gave her a small Arab, which is what she rode as a girl, because he believed that riding Shetland ponies made girls bandy-legged and there was no way any daughter of his would run that risk. As a result Olive never had to graduate from ponies to horses.

As a child and young girl Olive was an impish character, full of fun and always looking for adventure. She climbed into a baker's cart once, somehow locked herself in, and paid dearly for it by the terror she experienced at being locked up in the dark. Another day she climbed a ladder which had been left resting against a water butt. She reached the top, leaned over and lost her balance. Into the water she went. Fortunately the barrel was full, and Olive was able to cling to the top until help came.

Her mother made a big fuss on this occasion and insisted on looking after Olive herself, rather than letting the servants do so, which was the usual thing. She rushed Olive into the day nursery on the ground floor, put some milk on to boil and went upstairs to get some blankets. As if nearly drowning herself was not enough for one day, Olive up-ended the boiling milk over her throat while her mother was upstairs and nearly scalded herself to death. No wonder that she described herself as a little monkey when she was a girl.

Olive and her brother had four governesses, all from the continent. Marguerite was the first and, as the name indicates, she was French, as was "Little Rose", one of the maids. As a result Olive and John ended up with a good grasp of French. In fact, one of the reasons for employing foreign governesses and maids was so that the children would grow up speaking French and German naturally.

Marguerite was followed by a German girl, Fräulein Schmidt, but she did not last long. The two children did not like her Prussian style, and played up so badly that she was soon asked to leave. The streak of determination that Olive displayed in later years was not long in coming to the fore.

Mlle Jaggi was next, and the children got on famously with her. Last of all was Mlle Joska, a Polish girl. She could speak French and German fluently, so as a girl Olive was able to speak and follow these two languages as well as Polish.

Shelley Lodge, the family home, was right next to the Convent of the Sisters of Our Lady of Sion, and that in turn was next to the Catholic Church, St Mary of the Angels, in Gatwick Road. The home was two-storeyed, and Olive was intrigued by the view she had from upstairs, of the nuns going to and fro, especially at those times when they were moving two by two into the chapel.

Olive's family was not very religious. They did go to church occasionally, but this seems to have been more a matter of form than inspired by deep conviction. If William

and Ethel Edden were not religiously inclined, the governesses to whcm Olive had been entrusted were, and they
seem to have had a great influence on her in this regard.
Indeed, the governesses were a major formative influence in
shaping Olive's character, and she was greatly blessed to
have lived with such loving, caring women. They were not
merely devoted to her; they were upright women whose
example of genuineness and goodness spoke to her far more
eloquently than any sermon. The fact that they all happened
to be Catholic was accidental, but this doubtless had a great
deal to do with Olive's embracing Catholicism later in life.
The fact that God was a living reality to these women
communicated itself to Olive, and there was awakened in
her a consciousness and an awareness of God that was to
grow and deepen throughout her life.

Over seventy years later, sitting in her room in Madras on
the eve of the feast of Corpus Christi, she wrote into her
book of *Jottings* the impression this feast had made on her
as a child:

This was my first encounter with a Catholic feast day. I
must have been about six years old the first time I saw the
procession from our nursery window which overlooked
the garden of the Catholic schools . . . .

The banners, the priest under a golden canopy, the
altar boys, the acolytes, the incense, the singing, the long
line of little boys in white suits each escorting a little girl
who looked like a bride with a white veil, white dress and
blue sash, then the congregation all winding their way
through the garden past the first class tennis courts . . .
into the church.

Mademoiselle took me there once . . . . It smelt so nice,
and there were lots of flowers and white lace and the
clergyman was in a beautiful green dress with lots of gold
in it . . . .

How I wish I could go more often. I even think I might be good.

What was happening to Olive in all of this? Was God reaching out to her, arousing in her a yearning for Himself in a genuine experience of the divine, or was she merely swept up by beautiful ceremonial and ritual into a state of religious fervour that went as quickly as it came without having any permanent significance? We do not know. What we do know is that seventy years later, when preparing to celebrate the same feast, Olive had come to a faith that was deep and enduring and that was not dependent on ceremonial and ritual.

In due course Olive began school at Seabury, a very well conducted school run by two Eurasian sisters. There were eighty pupils at this "School for the Daughters of Gentlemen", a title which invariably brought a chuckle from Olive in later life. She had been born and bred in the upper class and this left its mark on her, but she consciously eschewed any pretensions to the superiority that the terms "gentleman" or "lady" sometimes imply. None the less, she received a sound education amongst the "daughters of gentlemen" at Seabury and was well prepared to take her place at Roedean when the time came for her to move into the middle and senior secondary classes.

3

School life
at Roedean

Roedean is situated in Brighton which is about thirty miles
from Worthing. The school was established by three sisters,
Penelope, Dorothy and Millicent Lawrence. The decision to
begin the school was taken primarily to solve the family's
financial difficulties and to keep the family together. The
father, Philip Lawrence, had not been a success as a barris-
ter; he had suffered poor health for ten years and then had a
bad accident while climbing in Cumberland.

Faced with the problems of supporting the family and
educating the children – there were fourteen of them – his
wife Margaret turned their home in Wimbledon into a
school. She ran this with the help of the elder daughters and
barely managed to make ends meet.

Since there was no prospect of the situation improving,
Dolly and Millie suggested to Nelly that the three of them
set up a proper school. This they did by moving from
London to Brighton, little thinking that they were establish-
ing what was to become one of the most successful schools
in England. The beginning was modest – when they first
opened the doors of Wimbledon House School they had
only ten pupils, "six paying and four for show" (the four
included their younger twin sisters) but it grew quickly. The
three sisters became known as The Firm and they were
occasionally referred to as the "Triumvirate", which could

have been rather offputting to timid homesick girls having their first taste of boarding school life.

It was not like this, though. The three sisters consciously set out to create a homely atmosphere. The school had begun as a family affair and it developed as a family school. At one stage eight of the Lawrence sisters were teaching at Wimbledon House, and their way of looking at the school was as an enlarged family.

The enterprise proved so successful and the Lawrences gained a good reputation as educators so quickly that numbers mushroomed and larger premises were urgently needed. They moved to Arundel Terrace and Sussex Square initially, and fifteen years later moved again, this time several miles out of Brighton. They acquired eighteen acres from the Marquess of Abergavenny at Black Rock on a hillside overlooking the sea, where the Marina is now situated. Immediately to the west is the golf course, while to the east a further twenty-four acres subsequently became available. When the school moved to its new site it was renamed Roedean.

It was into this environment that Olive moved in the summer of 1912. She found herself with four hundred and fifty-six other students, but she did not have the impression of living in a big, impersonal institution. The main building was designed as four separate houses, each one planned to be as similar as possible. Each house mistress had her own drawing room and study as well as private accommodation. The girls in each house also had a drawing room and study, besides a preparation room, and they slept in bedrooms, not dormitories. For one term Olive had her own room, but most of the time she shared a room overlooking the sea with three other girls.

The dress worn by the girls intrigued Olive. One of the sisters, Sylvia Lawrence, designed the "djibbah", basing it on the clothing worn by North African tribesmen. The tunic-like garment with V-shaped neck back and front was worn over a chiffon blouse, and was an all-purpose dress worn in class and for drill and physical education.

Olive very much enjoyed her time at Roedean. There was plenty of academic work and the girls were encouraged to work hard. As Penelope Lawrence said in one speech, "You have come here not to learn any one particular thing but to learn to use your brains. I cannot give you more brains than you have, but I can teach you to use what you possess." The school reports of the time show that the subjects Olive studied were Bible History, English (literature, essay, grammar), Mathematics (arithmetic, geometry, algebra), Natural Science, Languages (French, German, Latin), Music and Aural Training, Geography, History and Physical Education (dancing and gymnastics).

It was unusual at the time for girls to do some of these things, and Roedean broke new ground in a number of areas. The school week was divided into sixty periods of forty minutes each, and everything was done within those periods, homework included. The day began with morning prayer at 8.30 and finished with the last period at 7.30 in the evening. The long day accounted for the complete disappearance of day scholars by 1912, since only the stouthearted could face coming to school on a day-to-day basis with hours as long as that; and in any case, the homes of day scholars would have had to be very close to the school as well.

Olive did not mind the regime, in fact she revelled in it. She was an average student and did reasonably well in most subjects, but there was room for improvement in some areas. A comment of her gymnastics teacher enables us to imagine what Olive was like: "Good energetic work spoilt by lack of control."

17

Besides academic work there were activities of all sorts. There had to be, to keep over four hundred girls out of mischief! So Olive played tennis, lacrosse, hockey and cricket. She liked lacrosse best of all, but was happy to play cricket too. Christabel and Theresa Lawrence had enjoyed a reputation for being demanding cricket coaches in their day, while in Olive's time the girls were coached by an Essex cricketer, formerly a Test player. Regular matches were played against Dartford Physical Training College and Wycombe Abbey. The annual Fathers' Day Matches were a highlight, and having Roedean daughters pit their skills against their fathers at cricket was so unusual that it was featured as a cartoon in *Punch*.

Carpentry was another unusual activity for girls in those days, and on the occasion of his visit to the school Baden-Powell expressed surprise at the quality of the work produced by the girls.

The varied curriculum and extra-curricular activities stimulated Olive and increased her natural curiosity. She admired and respected Miss Penelope Lawrence, whom she saw as the natural leader in the school, and described her as rather Edwardian. However, Olive was not overawed. Her impish spirit broke out in a number of ways and she organized several midnight parties with a few of her cronies. Renovations to the swimming pool were being made at the time, and some of the corrugated iron fencing was removed. This gave access to the pool, so Olive was quick to take advantage of it by organizing her parties at the poolside and, what is more, was never found out.

She was not so lucky one night when she and her companions were involved in horseplay in their bedroom. At one point Olive threw the nightdress of one of the girls out of the window — and of course it would have to land on the shoulders of the Rt Hon Sir Paul Ogden Lawrence Q.C., as

he walked below! (Paul was the brother of the three Lawrence sisters; it was he who gave them the first loan which
enabled them to begin Wimbledon House School, and he
kept a keen interest in Roedean until his death.)

On another occasion Olive led a group into the fields for a
night picnic and nearly set a haystack on fire, reminiscent of
the huge bonfire lit at the school years before to celebrate
the relief of Mafeking. That had brought several horse-
drawn fire engines on site, for the townsfolk thought that
the school must have been going up in flames.

After two terms boarding Olive was summoned home.
Her father's health was failing and it was obvious that he
would not last very long. The First World War had sorely
taxed him – three of his four sons had been killed, and only
Harold survived. Once he realized that he was dying he
wanted to have Olive near him, so she went home immediately. It was not an easy situation, for her father was often
delirious and in that condition he confused Olive's mother
with his first wife. He turned against her for some reason
and she could do nothing for him, so it fell to Olive's lot to
bring him his meals and nurse him through his last illness.
When he died in 1919 at the age of seventy-seven she
experienced the grief that any daughter who loves her father
goes through, but she recognized that it was a merciful
release and she had no regrets. In those days it was not
customary for girls to go on to the cemetery for a funeral,
but Olive did. Though she was present as her father's
remains were lowered into the grave, she did not shed a tear,
having determined beforehand not to cry, and she managed
to contain herself. Throughout her life Olive did not like to
show her feelings, though perhaps it would have been better
had she done so. Was this a case of showing "the stiff upper
lip"? It certainly did not mean that there was any lack of
affection – Olive loved her father very dearly.

William Edden had likewise been extremely fond of his youngest daughter. She had been born to him late in life, when he was sixty. As a result when she was growing up he was unable to do with her many of the things parents enjoy doing with young children. He would, for example, have loved to go riding with her but had to settle for driving a coach-and-four instead. One of Olive's proudest childhood memories was in fact driving Lord Lichenfield's coach-and-four when she was eight years old. And her father was equally proud of her achievement.

After his death Olive went back to Roedean and had two more years there. She loved to browse, and at this stage spent many pleasant hours in the well-stocked library of the school. She often snuggled into an armchair at a window overlooking the sea and was lost in a world of fantasy and romance. One of the books she read there and later remembered having been fascinated by was *Swiss Family Robinson*. Another thrill for her was to go for a swim with the other girls on the private beach in front of the school. It was not quite so much the swim as the chance to go through the tunnel. This was quite an experience, for in 1910 a passage-way had been fashioned from the edge of the playing fields, under Brighton Road, right down to the beach. One hundred and fifty-four steps on a very sharp gradient led right through the cliff face, and a trip down these could conjure up all kinds of fantasies: "What a place for pirates to hole up in! And smugglers! And even Roedeanians! What a smashing place for a midnight picnic if only you could get in. The trouble was the iron grille gates were always securely locked at both ends. If only there was some way of getting hold of the key. But that too was always left out of harm's way. Miss Lawrence always saw to that. There would be no danger of setting fire to anything in there – no haystacks to get out of control. Never mind! We'll just have to make do with the swimming pool."

In her last two years at school, Olive must have shown some degree of responsibility for she was made a house prefect. She was also in the Swimming Club and the House Cricket First Eleven.

During this time her half-brother Harold used to visit her occasionally. He was considerably older than she, was a Major in the Army and had served in India. More important, he had a car that Olive thought was Christmas and Easter rolled into one. Recalling with relish the drives she took with him she would say, "I felt like the cat's whiskers", and she re-lived the pleasure of those hours at the mere memory of it all. The car, a Dion de Bouton, was black with gold fittings and had a criss-cross pattern painted over it, just the thing to make a young lady feel that the world was at her feet.

Harold sometimes drove her home on these occasions, but she also liked taking him to the Long Furlong on the Downs. This was just outside Worthing, not far from Arundel, and it was a favourite spot of Olive's. Her father used to drive her out there in a dogcart so that she could pick flowers in the fields, especially harebells and cowslips.

A dewpond on top of one of the hills had been a frequent haunt when Olive went off for picnics there with Tiny, later to be the Duke of Norfolk, and his three sisters, Ladies Rachel, Catherine and Beatrice.

Picking cowslips with the Norfolk family was now a thing of the past, but she did go hunting with them, and she was now at the stage when she used to join them when balls were being held. In her old age she described herself as having spent a frivolous youth, but it was all innocent fun, and in time Olive came to see the serious side of life.

Romance came into her life for the first time – but by no means the last – while she was at Roedean. In her last year she met Richard Fallowes when she was home on holiday. She accompanied her mother to afternoon tea with Mrs Fallowes and Richard happened to be home from Cambridge. They immediately hit it off together and Olive was quite taken by this young, very handsome undergraduate. Soon after, Richard visited Roedean with Olive's mother and all three had a "study tea". They saw one another regularly after that, and in a short time Richard presented Olive with an emerald surrounded by diamonds and asked her to marry him. Olive was swept off her feet, so when Richard went on from Cambridge to a theological college in Dorchester to prepare for the Anglican ministry she travelled to Dorchester and spent several days there. Olive was chaperoned by her mother all this while, but she was so näive she did not even realize that she was being chaperoned. When it became obvious that Richard and Olive were serious about each other, Olive's mother began to take things into her own hands. She was convinced that Olive was too young to marry, and that her current behaviour was too wild for the wife of a clergyman. Something had to be done about both matters, and the solution was easy to come by. Why not take Olive on the Grand Tour?

4

The Grand Tour

William Edden had not been a great traveller. His principal interest had been building up his fortune through investment on the Stock Exchange. He had lived on an estate in Ireland outside Cork for some years, but sold this before the potato famine and set up in Portsmouth on a property large enough to run twenty horses. Then came the move to Worthing, where Olive was born and brought up. For him there was more than enough to occupy his attention in England, without worrying about roaming around the Continent.

Not so for Harold, his brother. Uncle Harold had travelled extensively in Europe with a tutor when he was a young man, and he was an enthusiastic tourist. He knew what hotels to stay at, where to go and what to do, and it was he who suggested the itinerary that Olive and her mother followed. France, Belgium, Holland, Germany, Austria, Switzerland and Italy were taken in, and the usual attractions, from the Eiffel Tower to the Isle of Capri, were visited, appreciated and post-carded.

Wherever they went Olive wrote back to Richard every day, and from these letters he compiled a comprehensive diary of the journey. For most places the diary read like excerpts from Baedeker's Guide, but at several points they went off the beaten track and not even Baedeker could match some of their exploits.

Jaggi, one of Olive's governesses, was living at Lyons. So Olive and her mother forsook the five-star hotels and stayed with her. A foray into the local market was an experience Olive remembered vividly, especially the stall that sold nothing but snails. Copper pans eight by twelve inches were indented all over to carry patty pans, in each of which sat a snail cooking away in butter and herbs. "Delicious", was Olive's verdict, and down they went, one after another.

From Lyons to Marseilles, then they took a boat to Algiers. For nearly three months they were in North Africa, and her Olive really came alive. The cathedrals and museums of Europe had been fascinating enough, the mountains and glaciers of the South Tyrol were breathtaking, riding the patchwork of canals in Venetian gondolas was unforgettable, but what could touch the Arab world for exotic adventure?

Lawrence of Arabia had discovered this very world not so long before, and Olive could imagine herself riding out to adventure with him over the sand dunes.

Lawrence did not materialize, but the French Foreign Legion did. From their hotel in Algiers, Olive and her mother travelled to Bousaida in the Sahara. A detachment of legionnaires were stationed here, and Olive went riding with them when they were exercising their horses, or at least she did until they were summoned into the desert on a punitive expedition. Olive no longer had her escort, but such considerations never daunted her, and she continued to ride. But her lack of experience in the desert played her false and one day, before she knew it, she was lost. Not only lost, but fearfully hot and rapidly becoming dehydrated. She dismounted, fell asleep in the sand and, while she was asleep, her horse wandered off. Meanwhile a wind had sprung up and the hoofmarks were obliterated. None the less she managed to get back to the palm trees again, and later realized that when she had been on the horse she had gone around in a circle.

24

Some Bedouins arrived, but even then Lawrence of Arabia did not materialize! The Arabs treated her kindly and discovered what her predicament was. It was too late to get her back to Bousaida that day so they made her welcome for the night in one of their tents. Goats, chickens, children, adults – all were in together, but Olive was relieved to be safe and sound and was happy to sleep on the hessian bags spread out for her in a corner of the tent. She was not so happy to be given, as a special delicacy before she went off to sleep, a serving of sheep's eyes. According to local custom these were swallowed whole, so down they went, but Olive was not as appreciative of these as she had been of the snails at Lyons. The next morning the Bedouin sent one of their number ahead to alert Olive's mother that all was well, and a few hours later accompanied Olive back to the hotel. She was less distraught than her mother, in fact it was all rather exciting to look back on now that she was out of danger. But she did have an added respect for the desert after this, and grateful affection for her Bedouin rescuers.

Tunis and Carthage were next on the itinerary, and it was while at the thermal springs of Hamen Meshitien, with its hot waterfalls, that they tried the local chicken. At least, chicken is what the menu said, but they later discovered that they had just had their first meal of monkey!

On to Egypt and the more reliable menus of Mena House at the oasis near the pyramids. Here, however, some of the camel drivers were not so reliable. The ten-minute ride from Mena House past the pyramids and on to the Sphinx can be a memorable experience, not only because of these wonders of the ancient world just yards away, but also because the camel drivers may ask for baksheesh. If a good tip is forthcoming all is well, but if not the driver gets the camel to break into a trot – and for inexperienced tourists this can be very unnerving. No wonder the prudent ones go in horse-drawn drags. You can imagine Olive's choice though, even if it meant a temporary separation from her mother.

A boat trip down the Nile completed their Egyptian sojourn. Then they picked up a ship returning from India via the Suez Canal and travelled to Sicily. In the few days here Olive had an encounter which stayed with her throughout her life. She had been up to see Mt Etna, and it was on her way down that she saw a priest labouring up the hill. There were a number of villages in the region and they had all looked drab and cheerless. There was not a blade of grass to be seen anywhere – and the total absence of foliage added to the depressing atmosphere that the whole scene engendered. Evidence of grinding poverty was on every side, and the priest himself was obviously living in straitened circumstances. His soutane was greyish green with age, his boots were badly scuffed, the leather in the toes were grey for want of bootpolish, and the shovel hat perched on his head completed the picture of what could have been a pitiful figure. Yet when he drew near to Olive he raised his hand as if in blessing. His face lit up with a radiant smile, and he exuded such happiness that Olive was dumbfounded. How could he experience such happiness in such depressing surroundings? Not a word passed between them. The encounter lasted but a few seconds and then he had passed. But the impression was so vivid and the impact so lasting that even sixty years later Olive could recall every detail.

For Olive that was a privileged God-moment. There seemed no earthly reason for the priest's happiness. In the years that followed, the memory of that incident would occasionally flash through her mind and with it a sense of the presence of God that she had experienced at the time. To her it seemed that the priest himself enjoyed a deep sense of union with God. There had been no need to speak – God had reached out to Olive through him. He had touched her, ever so gently but ever so deeply.

Embarking at Messina, they took ship for Naples and successfully avoided both Scylla and Charybdis, of which Olive had learnt when studying Latin. The Blue Grotto at Capri, the Amalfi Drive from Sorrento, the Palace of Caserta which had been built to rival Versailles, the ruins of Pompeii – all these kept Olive and her mother occupied while based in Naples. Then Rome with all its attractions, the Forum, the Villa Borghese, the Vatican Museums and the Sistine Chapel, the Villa d'Este at Tivoli, with its gardens and fountains. After that it was Florence, with all the treasures of the Pitti and Uffizi Galleries, the buildings and statues of Michaelangelo, especially the masterpiece of David in the Accademia, the Duomo and Giotto's famous bell tower and, last of all, the Baptistery.

Olive had been to many, many galleries and had seen some of the greatest works of art the Western world has produced, but the most vivid impression she retained of all this was a little squirrel depicted on the doors of the Baptistery in Florence. Ghiberti's gold doors, with their exquisite figures showing characters and incidents from the Bible, are so magnificent that they have been declared worthy to be the Gates of Paradise itself. And what did Olive remember from it all? A carving of one of God's creatures frolicking in the sunshine. She herself said that it was as though God was speaking to her in this way, giving her an appreciation of the simple things of life. She had always been surrounded by affluence, she was completing a tour of over six months, mixing with people in the very best hotels, seeing and having the best that money could buy, visiting places that only the well-to-do could get to in those days. So what tales does she carry home with which to regale her friends? Nothing more than a sorry-looking priest in Sicily, and a little squirrel in Florence sculpted in gold?

The memory of the squirrel on Ghiberti's doors came back to Olive sixty years later, when she had a real squirrel in her hands which took her thoughts to God just as effectively as the gilt one had done in Florence. The extract below is part of a prayer she wrote in Madras entitled, "Thoughts Raised by Half an Ounce of Fluff":

> Sweet Jesus, You who have tried to teach the world the true meaning of Love, Love so enveloping, so permeating it reaches to the very depths of man's soul.
> My God! The Trinity that I adore
> I thank You for all the loves of my life:
> My parents and the friends of my childhood and girlhood.
> My husband – it was through him that I just came really to know and to love my God.
> My children, my grandchildren, the friends of my later years.
> Though few of them knew it, I was being led nearer and nearer to my greatest love of all: Jesus, my Lord, my God, my All.
> The poor children of an Indian slum, the orphans and children of leper parents. I love them all, and because I love them, I find myself growing nearer and nearer to You. I look at my tiny pet squirrel, nestling in the palm of my hand; it is sleeping peacefully. It has confidence in me. It knows my hand from any other.
> Yesterday I thought I had lost it and only then did I realize that I loved that little scrap of fluff.
> Dear God, sometimes You seem to far away, my adoration so torpid. I am almost led to despair . . .
> "Lord I am not worthy." Of course I am not worthy, not even as worthy as that little squirrel, because I have not

even the trust that it has in me. I have only to clench my fingers and it would be dead, but I love it and could not do it.

How inconceivably greater is God's love for me!

5

Oxford House and romance in Denmark

When Olive returned from her trip Richard began dancing attention upon her once again and wanted to set a date for their wedding. He had everything arranged on his side, all that was needed was for Olive to settle on the exact time. Olive did not do this, but went instead to Oxford House in Bethnal Green. She realized that she did not know a great deal about real life and she wanted to do something useful for a change. She also wanted to learn more about God and the things of God. If she were to marry Richard she would have to know God better herself.

Her involvement with Richard had led to an increased awareness of spiritual matters. He was three years older than she, a very serious person, and he set Olive thinking much more than she had ever done before. With his encouragement she began reading a great deal, and together they read the New Testament. She had never read the Epistles of St Paul before, and she came to the New Testament now with new eyes. In her old age she was grateful to the various people who had enabled her to see things in a new light, and Richard was one of the most significant people in bringing this about.

Oxford House was conducted by Miss Havergill for the Church of England. She was very committed to the Church, was a well-known hymn writer, and lived a community-style life with the girls there. They had a chapel on the premises and used to come together to recite morning and evening prayer. Olive relished the opportunity to pray together regularly with others, and the Scripture readings that were part of this kept her mindful of God.

Helping the poor was their principal work and this took various forms. Many of the people in the slums had never had a holiday in their lives. Making it possible for them to get away for a short break was one thing, finding jobs for the unemployed, getting food for the destitute, providing medical care for TB cases, were other things they did.

Keeping track of all who needed help involved a considerable amount of paper work, for which Olive was in part responsible. She used to walk through the slums to the office in Hackney where this was done, and it was common enough for youngsters to ask for a penny. Olive knew what pennies were, of course, and so avoided the problem experienced by one of her companions. This was a Japanese girl who, when asked by youngsters for pennies on Guy Fawkes' Day, began distributing one and two shilling pieces, thinking they were half-pennies and pennies. In no time she was surrounded by a clamouring mob, and she only just managed to get away from them by getting through the Judas gate of Oxford House.

Olive enrolled in a course for social workers at Bedford College, affiliated with London University, while she was at Bethnal Green, and divided her time between her work with the poor and her studies. She made a number of friends at Oxford House – the Japanese girl affectionately known as Mlle Tokyo Sahn, two Danish girls and Lady Catherine Phipps, who renounced her title when she began working with the poor.

In the meantime, Olive had told Richard that she needed more time to think about getting married. While at Roedean she had "fallen in love with love", to use her own words, and the prospect of getting married was very romantic for a girl as young as herself. But as she gained some experience she began to have doubts about it all. Richard was head over heels in love with her and would have given her the world, but for Olive this was the sticking point. Richard pandered to her – "he would have given me the top brick off the chimney" – and she knew instinctively that it would not work out. She wanted someone, she *needed* someone, who could stand up to her, someone who had a mind of his own and would not invariably and inevitably fall in with her whims and desires. Richard was most upset, and Olive was too, for she felt very keenly about hurting him, but she knew in her heart of hearts that it was the only thing to do.

In 1925 Olive was invited to spend the summer in Denmark with the family of the Danish girls she had come to know at Oxford House. Mlle Tokyo Sahn also wanted Olive to go to Japan, but Denmark was more manageable and that is where Olive ended up. The Beckers family lived at Ussens on Fuhn, an island near Sweden, and Olive stayed here for the first month. The father was a minister and his church was near the rectory.

At the end of the month, Olive was preparing to go home when she was asked by a Mrs Greta Maurier to stay with her family for several months so that they could learn English from her. She did this, and in the ensuing months found she had two ardent suitors. Greta's brother had a yawl and organized to sail a group of people around Jutland. Olive was one of the guests, as was the eldest son of the Rosencrantz family. We do not know whether this young man was connected in any way with the Rosencrantz who figures in *Hamlet*. What we do know is that the Rosencrantzes were a prominent Catholic family in Denmark, and in their eyes it was essential that anyone marrying into the family be Catholic. The trip around Jutland lasted a week, and gave Olive and young Rosencrantz the opportunity to get to know one another. They enjoyed each other's company and were attracted to one another. However, Olive would not consider becoming a Catholic and nothing came of it, even though they did at one stage talk of becoming engaged.

The next suitor was rather more successful and brought Olive to the very door of the church. But he too failed to get her over the threshold, and never managed to slip on the wedding ring. Francis Chudoba was his name and he was the professor of history at Vienna University. Olive was on a visit to Stockholm and was in the Cathedral when Francis arrived with a group of young men, to whom he gave an explanation of what was in the Cathedral. Olive was fascinated and fell into conversation with him later. Shortly afterwards they met again by accident when they were on a boat going through the Goethe Canal. The trip lasted two days and there was plenty of time for them to talk, especially as they were able to get off the boat and walk together along the bank while the boat was going through the locks. They were talking in German all this time, for Francis did not have a good command of English. He now had plenty of incentive to learn, for with him it had been a case of love at first sight. He was so smitten that when the time came for them to part at the end of the two days he told Olive, "I will come to see you in England in a year, and by that time I will be able to speak English."

Olive went home to Worthing in due course, and true to his word, Francis turned up twelve months later. He did not announce that he was coming, but just turned up. Olive was having a holiday in Wales at the time and received a telegram from her mother: "Come home. Francis has arrived." Olive flew back home (not literally, for commercial plane services did not yet exist, but if she had had her way that would have been a possibility). As a girl she had a fascination for flying and would love to have done what Amy Johnson achieved. Her father knew how adventurous Olive was and would not give her the money to take flying lessons – he preferred to keep Olive grounded and alive rather than flying across oceans making a name for herself and probably preparing her own watery grave.

By the time Olive arrived at Worthing, Francis had captivated her mother and he was not long in captivating Olive too. In no time at all it was arranged that Olive should go to Vienna and enrol there in a course at the University.

6

Student life
in Vienna

It was ironical that Olive, who had rejected the idea of marrying Rosencrantz because he was a Catholic, was now being courted by Francis who had at one time seriously considered becoming a Benedictine monk. Coming from a family in which religious practice was more nominal than real, Olive had gone through a significant religious development. Her governesses had been people to whom religion had been important. Roedean had fostered in Olive spiritual values through chapel services and classroom teaching in Bible history. The Lawrence family had been nonconformist Unitarians, but the school services were conducted in the Anglican tradition, the chapel being the responsibility of Dorothy Lawrence, who was herself an Anglican. Religious tolerance was a feature of Roedean life then as now, and Olive grew up in an atmosphere which can be gauged from this extract from the School prospectus:

> While recognizing the need to help and encourage girls to form their own religious commitment, the School has always maintained a tradition of religious tolerance. For this reason girls of all Christian denominations and other faiths are welcomed. Christians are expected to attend either Chapel or an alternative place of worship on Sundays. Arrangements are made for Roman Catholic girls to attend Mass on Sundays at a local church, and instruction is available for those of the Jewish faith.

Into all of this came Francis. Olive's going to Vienna took her into a Catholic world. She had an apartment in Bergasse and was near the Votiv-Kirche, which she used to frequent. This had been built by Franz-Josef as a thanksgiving offering for his escape from an assassination attempt in 1853. The apartment was in the house of an impoverished baroness. Olive had a bedroom and two living rooms. The bedroom was the smallest of the three rooms, but it was three times bigger than an ordinary room, big enough to seat twenty couples. There would have been plenty of opportunities for Olive to have entertained this number, for she soon got to know a circle of friends amongst the students and they were often together.

Life in Vienna was a dream. There was the study, of course, and philosophy and history took up some of her time. But there were always the weekends, and Vienna being what it was there was constantly something interesting happening. In the home city of the Strauss family there were balls a-plenty, and Olive's love of dancing was amply satisfied. She had begun ballet while at Roedean and continued taking classes now. She was not quite in Dame Margot Fonteyn's class, and it is doubtful whether Rudolf Nureyev would have chosen her to partner him, but she was quite an accomplished ballerina. This often surprised people who knew her only later in life, when she had put on weight and it would have been difficult to imagine her flitting across the stage doing pirouettes and arabesques.

Olive's love of dancing went back to her childhood. While her mother was having breakfast in bed Olive would often put on an impromptu dancing show for her. At Seabury School in Brighton Miss Parkes taught her various steps, but this was not very thrilling. It did give Olive a few ideas of her own though and she used to improvise quite happily. At Roedean she was not at all impressed with the dancing mistress, Miss Idle, so was delighted on reaching Vienna to find herself steeped in a tradition of all that she believed dancing should be. She joined the White Russian Club, which had a goodly sized hall on top of a cafe on the west side of St Stephen's Cathedral. The members used to entertain one another with song and dance, and if there were an interlude in a set programme people were free to get up and dance. Olive often availed herself of this opportunity as well as taking part in regular performances. She danced in *Swan Lake*, and the president of the club was approached by Mme Karswima to see whether Olive would accompany her to the United States. Olive's commitment to Francis precluded this, but the incident gives an idea of the talent she did have.

Olive had seen the Champs-Elysées and been suitably impressed at the time of her Grand Tour, but the Ring-strasse was *her* street. She was a temporary Viennese and she relished the beauty of her adopted city.

The graceful living and the courtly manners of the Vien-nese — as in one form of greeting from a gentleman to a lady, "Küss die Hand, gnädige Frau" (I kiss your hand, gracious lady) — made a great appeal, especially with Francis at her side all the time to introduce her to the various attractions of the city. It was still 1928 and before the Depression. It was also before Hitler's *Putsch*, so life went on in a carefree, happy way. What could be more delightful than a meal in one of the *Heurigers*, those lovely little inns on the fringe of the Vienna Woods, or an evening at the Spanish Riding School to see the virtuoso performances of the Lipizzaner dancing horses.

Opera was another of her loves and she often bought a ticket for the *Stehplatz*, the cheap standing room section at the back of the stalls, or up in "the gods" where there were seats which she and most of her student companions who were also on allowances could afford. She was treated to the luxury of a box on the two occasions her mother visited her in Vienna. While she was studying Olive did not have a lot of money. Her mother gave her an allowance but quite deliberately saw that she did not have money to splash about. She learnt to make what she had go a long way. For that reason she used to eat in the students' restaurants where she got good meals at cheap prices. During the Emperor's time, what was left from his table used to be sent around to the students, but that was before Olive's day.

In 1928, the second year of her course, the centenary of Schubert's death occurred and there was a feast of concerts to attend. One of the events she recalled from this time was the commemoration of *Lilac Time*.

Living in Vienna in the shadow of the Hofburg and passing by magnificent buildings every day, she could not help but absorb a feeling for the architectural beauties of the city. Going to and from the university she went along part of the Ringstrasse, the majestic two-and-a-half mile boulevard that encircles the heart of Vienna with its 187-foot carriage-way. The buildings dotted along the Ringstrasse, such as the State Opera, the Rathaus (Town Hall), the National Theatre, the Parliament, the Palace of Justice, the Stock Exchange, the Neue Hofburg, the Kunsthistorisches Museum and the Naturhistorisches Museum, are of such magnificence and are so tastefully set amongst spacious parks and gardens that they give the Ring a grandeur that is scarcely matched by any other street in the world.

Francis was not an academic whose world was solely that of books and operas, ballets and balls. He was a keen outdoors man too, and many a weekend was spent in the mountains tramping or skiing, depending on the season. One Easter a party of fourteen of them went off hiking through the mountains. Patches of snow remained in odd places they were walking through, but the paths were well defined and there was little difficulty. Olive enjoyed these walks and marvelled at the music of the bells attached to the necks of the cows. The bells varied in size from cow to cow, and so did the notes they produced. Every time a cow took a mouthful of grass the bell would tinkle, so when there were seventy or eighty cows grazing in close proximity on the one alp there was a delightful combination of tinkling bells, a Pastoral Symphony of a different nature from Beethoven's. Though she enjoyed the mountain treks immensely she was secretly afraid that one day she would have to do some real mountain climbing, for she had no head for dizzy heights falling away precipitously.

Then one day, sure enough, it happened. They were a day's walk from the railhead and had been on a well defined mountain trail that suddenly came to a ledge with a sheer drop of a thousand feet or more. There was a way forward but this was straight up, and could be traversed only by climbing up a series of iron rungs set into the rock face. The church and the houses in the valley below looked like matchboxes and Olive's knees started turning to jelly. However she did not want to be a spoilsport and force the others to retrace their steps. She told Francis that she was terrified, so it was agreed that he would go up immediately ahead of her and a friend would come behind. With her heart in her mouth she was helped on to the first rung and then it was up to her. There were about twenty rungs in all and they were surprisingly far apart. She edged her way up apprehensively, moving her left foot first from one rung to the one above and bringing her right foot up to join it. Rung by rung she advanced gingerly without daring to look down. She felt a great urge to jump away from the cliff and had never been more terrified in her whole life. The worst part was getting up the last two rungs. Francis and another young man held her under the armpits and hoisted her up on to the narrow ledge at the top from which she was able to get to the path. From that point on there was no difficulty but she was grateful that the party came down by another route. "Going up sheer rock faces was not my idea of enjoying myself", was her comment.

Skiing was something else that Olive learnt in Austria. It was not simply as a leisure pastime that she learnt this; it was a more practical necessity, as it was a means of getting from one place to another in winter time when otherwise she would have been snowbound.

Another pastime Olive *did* enjoy was canoeing. Her most memorable trip was a three-day expedition in spring down the Danube. Francis and two other friends accompanied her by train to Passau near the border of Germany and Austria. The Inn River joins the Danube at Passau, and with the waters coming down from the melting snow there was a good flow. They camped on the riverside, with cherry blossoms from a nearby orchard adding to the beauty. The next morning they were packing their gear into the canoes when two policemen came along to enquire what they were doing. On learning what they planned to do they tried to dissuade them, but Olive knew that Francis would not back out. The policemen pointed out the dangers but to no avail, so they took the precaution of getting the names of all four in case next-of-kin had to be advised. The Passau Cathedral is on a headland giving a good view of the river, and as the party set off they were waved farewell by worshippers emerging at the end of morning Mass. The venture did not strike Olive as particularly dangerous – there was no white-water canoeing involved. As a matter of fact, they created a few thrills for themselves by getting into the wash of steamers as they passed by, just to provide some variation from the placid waters they were canoeing in most of the time.

When they came to Melch they beached their canoes and gave themselves a break by looking through the Cathedral. Francis used to take opportunities like this to explain aspects of Catholic worship, much of which had been unfamiliar to Olive in Worthing.

During the time that she was studying in Vienna Olive twice went home to England to visit her mother, and on both occasions travelled by the Orient Express as far as Paris. She shared the experiences Agatha Christie brought to the world, but had no murder to report at the end of her journey. When Olive came to the end of her course in Vienna her mother began to get things moving. If Olive were to marry Francis, it was time to get things settled. She travelled to Vienna, helped Olive select a flat in the Imperial Palace, previously used for the Ladies in Waiting but at that time available to the public. Then there was the choice of wedding gown and a date to be fixed for the wedding itself. Her mother kept at Olive and insisted on pinning her down, and it was well that she did, for Olive came to realize that Francis was not the one she was to marry. She had been enjoying herself so much in all that Vienna had to offer that she had not faced the realities of life, nor what marriage to Francis would mean. After all, it was to be for life. Once again she knew that for her Francis was not Mr Right. Francis did not accept this and kept sending back to her the ring which she had returned – and which she was forced to return more than once – but Olive did go back to England and took up life in Worthing once again.

By this time Olive was going on for twenty-six. The two horses she had previously ridden, Silver King and Nugget, were still at Shelley Lodge, so she was able to get some pleasure out of riding. She also took up golf in earnest and was good enough to play for Essex. Another outlet was a girls' club for teenagers and young adults in the district. She helped run the club and was one of those who took these young people off on holidays, going to sites which were inexpensive, for these girls were not well off – they had considerably less than Olive.

Sunday School was another activity Olive involved herself in at this time. This did not last long though, for two of her boys were arrested and sent off to Borstal. Olive thought that she could not have been doing any good with the group, and so decided to give it up.

Instead of those activities, Olive returned to Oxford House in London. She resumed there the work she had done just over five years before, assisting the almoners in the hospitals of the district and bringing what help she could to the poor in the slums. In less than twelve months she was required back at Shelley Lodge, where her mother had taken sick and was no longer able to run the house. Olive took over this role and learnt something about house management. Little Rose, Olive's former nurserymaid, was still employed by the family. She had never married and now was a big help in keeping things running smoothly. Olive ordered what was necessary by way of provisions, but Little Rose did the actual cooking, so even at this stage Olive did not learn how to cook. She knew how to order the most exotic dishes, and could decipher the most complicated menus in French, but anything more than making a pot of tea or boiling an egg was beyond her culinary skills. In her current situation that made little difference, but all that was soon to change.

The ailing condition of her mother required Olive to be in Worthing but it did not shackle her to the house. She was free to join in the activities of the younger set, in fact she was the ring leader of the twenty young people who were always having parties, attending dances, organizing picnics or going for drives along the coast or into the Downs. Olive's usual companion on these occasions was a young man just back from China, and another couple in the group was Neville Allerton and a young lady recently arrived from the West Indies.

On the August Bank holiday in 1932 Olive's companion was unable to join her and the same happened with Neville's friend. "Well, I suppose we'd better go together", Neville said to Olive, and that was the beginning of a whirlwind romance that ended in marriage within two months. For ten years Olive had been all the time "going to get married", first with Richard, then with Rosencrantz and, longest of all – for four years – with Francis. But when the right man did come into her life she did not waste a moment.

Neville Allerton was born in Durham, but the family moved to Worthing where his father was at one time the town clerk. On finishing school Neville had begun a very good office job arranged for him by his father with the Far Eastern Oil Company. Six months of this was all he could take – Neville was not cut out to be deskbound, and he told his father he would soon be fearfully frustrated if he stayed on there. Instead of that he found a job for himself in the Snowy Mountains of Australia, where for over two years he was a jackaroo on a station which ran thousands of short-horns. The nearest town was Cooma, which in those days boasted a general store, two hotels and little else. Neville enjoyed the work and would willingly have stayed on, but drought struck, thousands of the cattle died, and all the unmarried men were laid off. Neville went to Broken Hill and scored a job with BHP shovelling coke into the blast furnaces. The work was crippling and was done in eight-hour stretches, but competition for jobs was so fierce that men were willing to break their backs if only they could hold down the job. The pressure was too great for one of Neville's companions, who put an end to it all by jumping into a cauldron of molten metal. Though he was only small, standing at five feet six inches, Neville was strong and hardy and he survived this unscathed. In time he returned to the UK, but England could not hold him, and before long he was in Ceylon working on a tea plantation as a creeper (a "creeper" was an apprentice learning the skills of managing a plantation). Palm Garden was the name of the place where he worked in Newralia, and things looked promising for Neville for the best part of three years, until the bottom fell out of the tea and rubber market. Again, Neville was laid off, and again he returned to England, this time aged twenty-four and without a penny to his name.

Neville's father was a lawyer, so he took on this son of his as an articled clerk, despite the fact that he had a restless, roving spirit. He drew the princely salary of two pounds ten shillings a week, less than Olive was getting as petty cash at the time, but he had to stick at it, for the world was at this point in the grips of the Depression.

It was just at this time that he came into Olive's life. They were kindred spirits, both alive to adventure of any kind, ready to tackle anything and willing to launch into projects without worrying about planning everything to the last tedious detail.

The very way in which they came to marry symbolizes much of what they did in later years. They had been going with each other for barely two months when, one Friday afternoon, while they were waiting at a garage as their car was being topped up with petrol, Neville turned to Olive and said, "Why don't we get married, Olive?" Olive was quite certain it was the right thing and without a moment's hesitation said "Yes".

The two conspirators swung into action immediately. Without breathing a word to anyone except their best friends, who were to act as best man and bridesmaid, arrangements were made. Since it was Friday they could not be married in less than two days, even with a special licence. The wedding reception was a simple affair to organize, for there were going to be only four people present. A picnic basket, including a bottle of champagne, oyster patties and a three-tier wedding cake, was procured and popped into the back of the car. The following Monday Neville and Olive met at the Littlehampton Registry Office – Littlehampton is the town next to Worthing and only a quarter of an hour away by car. There the knot was tied in very simple fashion, and the four of them then headed off to the woods of Arundel Castle. A picnic in the woods was their wedding reception. A policeman on a bicycle went by and Olive immediately invited him over for a glass of champagne and a cigar. He was given their Box Brownie camera and with that took the wedding photos, none of which came out.

It was about 4.00 p.m. that same day when Olive burst in on her mother at Shelley Lodge. She threw her bouquet into her mother's lap and said, "There you are! I'm married!" Her mother was speechless. All she could say was, "Oh, Olive!"

And so began, in this unlikely way and in such unpromising fashion, a marriage which was to last over forty years and survive numerous difficulties in three different continents. A young love had been sealed by the marriage bond, and was to become deep and enduring and bring much happiness to two adventurous souls who were to support and sustain one another through thick and thin. And there was to be plenty of both in the years ahead.

Once both families had recovered from the shock of what had happened they began to think it would be a good thing to do it all again properly and with due decorum, so that is what happened. A "proper" wedding was organized in Thomas à Becket's Church two weeks later and the ceremony solemnized by the Rev. Mr Godber. The church was packed, and a more appropriate reception was held. Now that everything had been done *comme il faut* Neville and Olive settled down to married life, something that would never have been allowed but for their subterfuge, for Neville had just begun his training as a lawyer and could hardly be expected to support a wife on the salary of an articled clerk, certainly not in the manner in which she had been accustomed to live.

7

Life at Findon
and the War

At the age of twenty-seven Olive's lifestyle went through a radical change. With the exception of the years in Vienna, where she had to watch the pennies carefully, she had always lived in great comfort and had everything that money could buy. Now she had to run a household on two pounds ten shillings a week, and she found herself responsible for the cooking and the cleaning, the washing and the mending. The servants of yesteryear were no more. Olive went through a rapid period of enforced domestication.

For a time after getting married Neville and Olive lived with Mrs Edden in the family home at Shelley Lodge. Jean was born in 1933 and Bill followed fifteen months later. With the arrival of the children a home of their own became more desirable than ever, and when Jean was five the family moved to Findon.

About ten miles out of Worthing, the village of Findon is located in a rural area where the abundance of trees and green fields gives it a delightful setting. The one principal road, High Street, wends its way past the newsagent and general store, then on to the local inn and a few shops which quickly give way to houses. A hundred yards further on is Artist's Cottage, built for the Scottish artist Holman Hunt by his aunt. This was procured for Olive and Neville and here they lived from 1938 until 1948.

Neville was very keen on animals and kept two marmosets or baby monkeys, named Inkity-Unkity and Somella. They also had a South American tree bear, Kotimundi, which escaped once and had to be brought back by the local policeman. Dogs and cats abounded, three or four of each helping make up the menagerie. Oddly enough, Olive was not a pet lover; it was Neville who was keen to have all these pets. With the coming of the war the animals were passed on to a private zoo.

There was a weekly trip into Worthing on Mondays to buy provisions, and this also meant a visit to Granny. Jean looked forward to these occasions, as she would join Olive and her grandmother after school, and it gave her the opportunity to play the grand piano in the smoking room.

Visits to Neville's parents were a regular thing, too. The Allertons lived on the seafront at 44 West Parade, and Grandpa Allerton went for a daily dip until he was eighty. The beach was mined during the war, and barbed wire entanglements were erected, which put paid to bathing and beach games "for the duration". Something set off one of the mines near 44 West Parade, close enough for it to blow the front windows out. No one needed further encouragement to keep off the beach after that.

If Neville was interested in animals and liked keeping pets, Olive was very much a people's person; she enjoyed company and related easily and well to people, even complete strangers. She never had any inhibitions about striking up a conversation with people at a bus stop or at a meeting, even if she had never laid eyes on them before. As a result, friends were always dropping into Artist's Cottage. When food became short during the war Neville's parents would cycle out from Worthing on a Sunday, and the two families would combine their meat rations so they could have a roast.

Neville kept at his study of law consistently, if not enthusiastically, and was about to take his final exams when war broke out on 3rd September. He had been an officer in the Reserve army, the Territorial Artillery, and on 4th September he was called up, and in no time was off to France with the British Expeditionary Force.

In the early months, during the "Phoney War" when nothing much was happening and the French felt secure behind their Maginot Line, letters came through from Neville quite regularly. But when the shooting began in earnest the field cards became much less frequent. Neville was away for over a year, and though he was drawing a Captain's salary Olive had little money with which to support the family.

Initially she knew nothing about gardening and did not know how to go about growing vegetables. However, there was plenty of ground available both in the Cottage garden and in the one attached to the large manor to which she had access. She rented out half of her own land to an Irish potato king, observed carefully what he did and she did likewise. In all, she had two acres to look after and soon she had a flourishing vegetable patch with all kinds of edibles growing there. There were a number of fruit trees in the garden which were bearing well too, so she was able to supplement the food supply for the family and neighbours quite significantly.

Olive wanted to do something really worthwhile for the war effort, and was frustrated at being tied down in Findon where all she could do was teach others what she had picked up herself. She was able to help some of the women who had difficulty planning their purchases of meat, in such a way as to make the ration go as far as possible. Though she had had little practical experience before she married, she learned quickly, and was able to adapt to new and changing situations more quickly than most of her neighbours.

Just before France fell Neville was involved in the withdrawal to Dunkirk. He got his men to the channel port without great loss, but he himself ran into trouble during the evacuation. With Stukas dive-bombing the heavy concentration of troops on the beach, getting his men safely on to anything that would float was a nightmare. No sooner did he get on board a ship than it was hit and he had to take to the water. In the scramble that ensued he was crushed between two boats and was left stranded in the water for four hours. Eventually he was hauled on board the *Codrington*, "pretty badly mashed up", as Olive later described it. The only things he managed to keep with him were his revolver and his tin hat.

The first Olive knew of all this was a phone call Neville made from Portsmouth to the local grocer about midnight. He in turn brought Olive to the phone and she was greatly relieved to learn that he was alive, though she was soon to learn that he was far from well. He asked her to bring clothes down to Salisbury, so she arranged for the grandparents to look after the children, packed up what clothes she could lay her hands on, and got the car out at 7.00 a.m. Luckily, it had a full tank, for petrol was hard to come by, so she was able to get to Salisbury by about lunchtime.

It had been two months since Olive had received any word from Neville. She had actually given up hope of ever seeing him again, so she was in seventh heaven when she found herself in his arms once more. But he was in very bad shape. From the time he had come back from the front until the evacuation, he had had no food. The only things of his own he had been able to save were his gold cuff links. The rest of his clothing was gone, the trousers and sweater he had on had been given to him on the *Codrington*. While he had been in the water there was constant bombing and strafing with machine gun fire and he was extremely lucky not to have been hit. His prolonged exposure to the cold autumn water left him marked for life, and he took no further part in active service during the war.

The sights that he had seen during the retreat were also to stay with him for life. Big numbers of lorries loaded with munitions were on the road, and every so often one of these went off with a huge explosion when it suffered a direct hit, taking everything in the vicinity with it, man, beast and material. The roads were clogged with refugees fleeing the battlefront, and the carnage amongst the civilians from the bombing was appalling. He experienced a rude shock as he made his way back to the staging camp near Dunkirk; he had sent a dispatch rider ahead to give word that they were coming, only to learn the disquieting news that the camp was in the hands of the Germans. An outflanking man-oeuvre brought them safely to the beachhead, but it all took its toll on their nerves.

That was now all behind, thank God, and there was time to rest and recuperate. Neville and Olive were put up by a Major and his wife who had a house on Salisbury Plain. Olive remained there for a week looking after Neville, then returned home to look after the children while Neville was hospitalized. He was kept in bed for three months and fed on boiled fish and milk, having developed a duodenal ulcer. On being discharged from hospital he was sent home to convalesce, and his condition can be judged from the fact that he spent another three months in bed there.

On returning to active duty, Neville was with a group preparing to go to West Africa. Olive kept urging him to report that he was still unwell, but Neville would have nothing of this. Matters were taken out of his hands when he collapsed and had to be rushed to hospital. The regiment went off to Dakar without him, and he spent the rest of the war doing office work, much of it in the north of England in Matlock Castle, which was not heated and subject to cold draughts. This did anything but help his condition, and ever afterwards he was very susceptible to the cold.

With the remnants of the British Expeditionary Force back home, and with France in German hands, Britain braced itself for the invasion. But first came the "softening up" process with the blitz of London and other cities. The Battle of Britain took place in the air rather than on the beaches, and the success of the RAF kept the German armies on the continent.

Olive was blissfully unaware of the maelstrom that was about to be unleashed, and she decided one day in late summer or early autumn to take the children blackberrying. It was forbidden for civilians to go into certain parts of the Downs, but Olive was undaunted by this. She knew a particularly good place for blackberries, and just because a war had been raging in Europe was scarcely sufficient reason to keep her and the children home on a pleasant sunny day. The parents of a family nearby were both involved in the war effort, and their two daughters aged about twelve were at a loose end during the school holidays. Olive invited them to come along, so the five of them set out, Olive with Jean aged seven, Bill five, and the two girls about twelve. They were some distance from the village but not yet at the grove where the blackberries were growing, when the sky suddenly filled with planes. There were fifty of them, some German and some British. Olive and the children were in an open field covered with sheaves of corn but too far from the trees to get any cover there. A farmer and a number of workers were harvesting the crop by hand, which accounted for all the sheaves in the field. There was very real danger of being machine-gunned where they stood, so Olive pushed each of the children into a sheaf of corn and camouflaged herself in one of the sheaves likewise. The planes wheeled and swooped on one another, firing machine guns and cannon whenever they could get one another in their sights. The dog fight went on for some minutes, the sky was black with planes – then they all disappeared into the distance, the centre of action moving some miles away from Findon. Olive took advantage of this to run for cover with the children into the woods where the blackberries were. Then the planes returned and the fighting went on. One of the planes that was brought down was so close to them as it plummeted to the earth that they could see the flames licking about the fuselage. Twelve German planes were shot down that day, and the RAF lost a comparable number. Olive had witnessed the beginning of the Battle of Britain. She could not complain of being frustrated by not being where the action was!

The farmer's son had armed himself with a World War I pistol as protection against any of the German airmen who had parachuted from their planes before they went down. He would have been in trouble if he had been found in possession of it, and with plenty of military personnel likely to swarm over the area to pick up the downed airman he thought it better to get rid of it. He unloaded it and passed it on to Olive. She took it back with her and thought she would scare off any Germans she might come across by keeping the revolver in sight. She knew nothing whatever of firearms, but thought it would be best if the gun appeared loaded. Her way of doing this was to stuff some rabbit droppings into the chamber!

Luckily, she did not come across any of the Luftwaffe trying to evade capture, although seven of the planes had been shot down within a mile of Artist's Cottage. Two of the Germans were later buried in a corner of the graveyard at the church in Findon. They were set apart on their own, and Olive used to put bunches of flowers on their graves. She did not think of them as enemies, but saw them as the sons of some mothers grieving in another country, as she would have grieved had she lost a son herself. This was but one example of the compassion that Olive so often demonstrated. Nationality, creed, colour, these made no difference to her. Her heart went out to anyone in need, in this case to the dead and their mourning relatives, unknown and unreachable except through a love that transcended jingoistic patriotic feelings.

The first day of the Battle of Britain was the most memorable for Olive. She was not caught out in the open again with a dogfight raging above, but it was not the last time she was near a battle in the skies. Soon after the blackberrying expedition the siren went and Olive got the children into the air raid shelter in the garden. The sky was again crowded with Spitfires and Hurricanes desperate to bring down the Junkers and Heinkels before they could reach London and unload their bombs. When Olive and the children emerged from the shelter half an hour later the large car park at the end of their drive was littered with the casings of expended bullets from the planes.

Findon itself was never bombed, because it was a tiny village of no consequence as far as the war effort was concerned. Later in the war a large area of the South Downs was given over to the Canadian Army who used the area for training and for practising manoeuvres, but that was well after the German bombers had been cleared from British skies.

While the blitz was on, though, the planes flew right overhead on virtually every mission. Only after the war did the reason for this come to light. A hospital in Worthing run by nuns had a big flat roof and on this was painted a huge red cross. Easily visible from the air, it was a conspicuous landmark for the German navigators, and they used to head for this to get a bearing on their target in London or elsewhere.

It would be ridiculous to claim that Olive did not experience fear during these incidents, but the one time when she was absolutely terror stricken was when the Doodlebugs were coming over. The V1 and V2 rockets began exploding in London and in the southern part of England towards the end of the war, and the Allies had no answer to them. The whine of the rocket could be heard from several miles away, and when the noise stopped this meant trouble – the motor had cut out and the rocket was on its way down, somewhere nearby. Neville was home at the time. A Doodlebug could be heard on its way, and then all was silent. Olive clutched Neville for dear life and together they waited for it to drop on them. It landed two miles away and the explosion ripped out a hole big enough to swallow up two houses.

On another occasion the air raid siren went. This time Olive and the two children were outside, away from the house, so Jean and Bill climbed on the embankment of the road and put up an umbrella they happened to be carrying.

"What are you doing with that?", Olive asked.

"We are taking cover", was the reply.

Olive kept herself as busy as she could during the war, and kept from worrying by her activity. The garden absorbed a lot of her time and energy, and raising chickens, ducks, turkeys and rabbits plus two pigs was therapeutic as well as eminently practical and a most welcome addition to depleted foodstocks.

Towards the end of the war, Neville came home again. His bout in hospital when he collapsed with a duodenal ulcer had been followed by a lengthy period at home when he needed constant attention. Every half hour he had to be given olive oil, with frequent drinks of milk throughout the day.

8

Post-War years

When he was discharged from the Army, Neville returned to his father's office in Worthing. He disliked the work but endured it because he had to support his family somehow. Jean was by now nearly thirteen and Bill eleven.

Before the War Neville had enjoyed life in Australia and Ceylon, but when he returned to England he could still cope with living there. After the war the situation was different. He suffered intensely whenever it turned cold, especially when a cold wind was blowing. Doctors told him the only solution was to leave England for a warmer country, and it came down to a choice between Australia and Africa. Friends from Nyasaland were home on a visit, and they influenced Neville and Olive to think seriously of going there. They made enquiries about buying a small tobacco plantation and were in contact with someone willing to sell. Then the owner's wife changed her mind about wanting to leave, so the deal came to nothing.

Attention then switched to Kenya. They knew the Deputy Commissioner of Police in Kenya; he was the son of an Anglican clergyman in a nearby village. But it was the coloured brochures of the country and of Kitale in particular which brought them to their decision. Sitting on the floor of their lounge in Artist's Cottage, the pictures of Mt Elgon festooned with cotton wool clouds against an azure blue sky, the fertile red soil supporting tall lush crops of maize, and to cap it all the polo riders on their ponies at Kitale Club, left a very favourable impression. From that moment on they were quite definite as to where they were going. It was not just Kenya, it was to the White Highlands, and to Kitale in particular. This was in marked contrast to James Stapleton who went to Kenya with his family at around the same time, was for a year at the Agricultural School at Nairobi, and then spent months searching out a suitable property before finding one in Burnt Forest not far from Eldoret.

Financing the venture was the first thing to consider. Olive's mother had died soon after the war ended and although she had been comfortably provided for in her husband's will, the huge fortune which he had amassed nearly all went to the eight children of his first marriage. Some money came to Olive, but on its own it was not nearly sufficient to set them up. Several hundred pounds had unexpectedly come Neville's way from Palm Garden, the tea plantation in Ceylon. It had traded itself into a sound financial position and sent the money to him in England as a bonus. There was some money due to Neville from the Army when he resigned his commission, and then there were the proceeds from the sale of Artist's Cottage. There was enough for them to buy a reasonably sized farm, up to a thousand acres, and to get a good start in their new land, but they would have to be careful how they outlaid their money.

The attitude of the various members of the family towards leaving England varied significantly. For Neville it was an absolute must, and he relished the prospect of finally being liberated from his lawyer's desk. Olive saw it as she viewed so many of the changes in her life – it was a challenge, an adventure, something to enter into wholeheartedly so as to get the most out of it. Jean saw things in a different light. She was fifteen and coming to the end of her schooling. The world of theatre, opera and ballet were just opening out before her. Just after the war, shows like *Annie*

Get Your Gun were all the rage, and Jean was getting caught up in all of this. She had been able to go and see Robert Helpmann in *Sleeping Beauty* in London, and now she was facing the prospect of life in the outback of Kenya near the border of Uganda, where she would be leading a life more like that of Annie Oakley, rather than being able to see such a life depicted in a stage musical. Bill was somewhat younger and had not yet developed these interests. Moreover, the things that could be done in Kenya in those days were more likely to appeal to a boy than a girl. Shooting game to provide meat for the pot came to be part of the routine and had its attraction, bringing satisfaction to a boy, but not so to a girl.

Preparations for the trip took some time. The furniture and belongings that they took to Kenya were packed into a big wooden crate, somewhat similar to the modern containers for shipping goods. The crate was big enough to serve as a garage for their vehicle when everything was unpacked, and they managed to get an incredible amount into it – glassware, dinner sets, pictures, piano, crockery, kitchen ware, books, everything but the proverbial kitchen sink. They bought a Land Rover just before leaving England and used this to drive to Dover, where they took the ferry to Oostende and drove on to Antwerp. Here the vehicle was loaded on board – somehow the crate got there too – and they were ready for their trip to Mombasa on the Belgian ship *Capitaine Lombé*.

9

Bound for Kenya

The vessel in which they set sail from the Flemish port on 19th September 1948, was a converted Liberty ship. It was now a cargo boat and had accommodation for twelve people. Food rationing continued after the war until 1950, so it was not surprising that the menu on the *Capitaine Lombé* was very limited. Meat was in short supply, but horse flesh was available and was served on board. Jean in particular was horrified at the prospect, and this made for an unpleasant beginning to a trip whhich she found distasteful in many ways. Others on the ship were not upset in the same way. Anglo-Saxons have a sensitivity in this matter which is not shared in Europe, where patients suffering from heart trouble are sometimes prescribed horse flesh. In Italian towns the sign *Macelleria Equina* (horse butcher) is not uncommon. For much of the journey Jean was sea-sick, and she welcomed the end of the four-week trip. Sanitary conditions were primitive, with toilets that did not flush satisfactorily. Fortunately the weather was good throughout and they did not run into any storms.

After passing through the Straits of Gibraltar the captain took the ship close to the Algerian coast. He had learnt that Olive had spent time in North Africa in her late teens, and he very obligingly gave the passengers a close-up view of the coastline. They could pick out individual buildings in Algiers, but not the hotel in which Olive had stayed. The days sailing through the Mediterranean were uneventful, and they entered the Suez Canal without incident. A stop at Port

Said brought them into contact with the world of vendors hawking curios and keepsakes, who plagued passengers travelling through ports in the Middle East or the Orient. Olive was well equipped to use the ploy of getting rid of them by speaking French, German or Polish when they pestered her in English, "You buy? Cheap price!" It came as a surprise to find urchins dressed in tatters, selling newspapers or trinkets, able to respond in English, French, German and Italian. Having to live by their wits and having contact with tourists travelling through the Canal gave them an incentive to acquire at least a smattering of these languages that would enable them to sell their wares.

The sixteen hours it took to get through the Canal to Suez itself went slowly. The ship moved along at less than half speed so as not to create a wash that would eat away the banks. The narrow sweet-water canal running alongside with fresh water looked anything but sweet, and the scenery was anything but attractive as they cruised through arid land on both sides. The convoy of ships of which they were a part, travelling south, came to the port of Suez where De Lesseps' canal opened out into the Bitter Lakes. Here a group of ships lay at anchor waiting for their turn to enter the canal and the time for a northbound convoy to begin its passage through the canal. The *Capitaine Lombé* did not tarry at Suez but headed on as soon as possible down the Red Sea. For three days they were in this waterway, which evoked visions of Moses leading the Israelites out of Egypt towards the Promised Land. During those three days they came to have considerable sympathy for Moses and his followers wandering through the desert, for the air was uncomfortably warm — even hot — and oppressive the whole time. With desert on both sides of the Red Sea the water retained its heat night and day, and it was no use going on deck even at night time "to get a breath of fresh air". Relief came only when they came out of the Red Sea altogether, for the *Capitaine Lombé* was not fitted with an air-conditioning system, which made the trip through the Red Sea more tolerable for people on passenger liners.

Two days were spent at Djibouti where a load of fertiliser was taken on board, and then it was full steam ahead for Mombasa. The last week of the journey around the Horn of Africa and down the coast of Somaliland was rather more pleasant. Once in the Indian Ocean they had the benefit of fresh sea breezes again and there was the prospect of journey's end. They would see the last of that curious sign in the toilet "Shanks the Push", and food more to their liking would be available.

Mombasa was a complete surprise to Olive when they finally arrived on 24th October. She had been expecting a harbour with a wharf or two, a few native huts and little else. The bustling port which had become the hub of maritime activity in East Africa had extensive wharves and docks, huge cranes and derricks for loading and unloading cargo, trains and trucks and all the equipment that a modern port required.

Their Land Rover was unloaded together with their household goods and possessions – three tons of them. These were left in storage until they had a property on which to set it all up. They took with them only what they needed immediately and packed these things into the Land Rover. Mombasa is built on an island and is linked to the mainland by a causeway.

As they had sailed along the coast the last few miles to Mombasa, they had seen the Nyali Beach Hotel in a setting of coconut palms less than a hundred yards from the water's edge. This was THE hotel in Mombasa in those days, and when Neville had the family all on board the Land Rover it was this he headed for. They had not had a holiday since before the war, and he was determined they would have a break before they set off for Kitale.

10

Vacation in Mombasa

Nyali Beach Hotel had been open for only eighteen months when they arrived. *The Mombasa Times* carried an article on the hotel just before it was opened, and included these lines: "Standing a little back from the Nyali Beach on a slight rise, it commands a magnificent view of glistening white sand and seen through a fringe of gently waving palm trees and beyond, of the creaming surf pounding over the reef which encircles Nyali."

Full board in those days cost approximately twenty pounds per month. The service and amenities were second to none, for the hotel had been built and was managed under the supervision of Mrs Eva Noon, a pioneer hotelier in Nairobi, who exacted the highest standards from her staff. The hotel had a resident orchestra which played nightly for the guests to dance beneath the palms. Coming to a new luxury hotel after war-time conditions and rationing in England, and following the spartan conditions on board ship, the family was in a veritable paradise.

The abundance and variety of food left the children goggle-eyed. Fish of all kinds was on the menu, crayfish was served daily, beef and steak were commonplace, and then there was the fruit. Mango, paw paw and avocado had been merely names to them, and while they knew of pineapple and banana it had been a long, long time since they had been able to get them in any quantity. The dark-skinned African waiters dressed immaculately in white uniforms with red sashes and turbans could have stepped right out of a technicolour film, and the dazzling white beach lined with coconut trees was the equal of anything they had seen in a film of the day, *The Road to Zanzibar*, with Bob Hope, Bing Crosby and Dorothy Lamour.

A coral reef ran parallel to the beach a mile or so offshore and could be reached on foot at low tide. They had endless enjoyment poking around the reef, collecting shells and conches, frolicking in the warm water for hours on end and watching the natives paddling out to sea in their outriggers to catch the fish which landed on their table the next day. The beach was firm underfoot, ideal for beach-ball and hand tennis, but they needed their dark glasses, for the sand was blindingly white in the sun, as it was formed from the disintegrating coral.

Excursions into Mombasa were popular. It was only a ten-minute drive and there were a host of things to see. The people themselves were interesting. There was a large Muslim component in the population, and the girls and women were heavily veiled, wearing the black yashmak over their dresses and keeping their faces covered except for their eyes.

The Arab quarter was near the Old Port, and the streets and houses dated from mediaeval times. Streets and lanes too narrow for motor vehicles had a charm all of their own, with art and craft work on display, and large earthenware jars of water at the doors of some houses inviting passers by to slake their thirst. The picturesque dhows with their cargoes being loaded or unloaded for African ports near and far made for interesting photos, as they rode at anchor, with Fort Jesus in the background.

Jean and Bill were fascinated with their visit to the Fort. It had been built in 1593 by the Portuguese, to guarantee their access to the best harbour on the coast of East Africa. They had a trading settlement at Malindi nearby, the security of which was being threatened by Turkish ships which began appearing in the area, and also by the Arab community of Mombasa which had been persistently hostile. Occupying two acres, with walls fifty feet high and parapets eight feet wide, it was set on solid coral so it would not be undermined and was virtually impregnable until the invention of explosive shells. It withstood a siege from 13th March 1696 until 13th December 1698, and succumbed only because plague decimated the defenders when relief troops from Goa unwittingly brought it into their midst. Jean and Bill were particularly impressed by the room to which one of the surviving Portuguese led a number of Arabs when the garrison finally surrendered. He had told them that there was a cache of gold there but he led them in fact to the powder magazine which he set off once they were all inside, blowing them and himself to smithereens.

Neville had come across Buddhist and Hindu temples while in Ceylon, but for Olive, Jean and Bill their stay in Mombasa exposed them for the first time to people of other cultures and religions. An Arab mosque was on a corner of one of the main streets, and the men could be seen at prayer five times a day, with the sound of the muezzin summoning them to worship unable to be ignored. A sizeable Indian population was the reason for the large Hindu temple also in the old quarter of the city, and a Jain temple too was in the same area. The Muslim influence was most noticeable along the coastal strip but the Allertons were to be in constant contact with Indian traders the whole of their time in Kenya.

After two weeks at Nyali Beach the time came to push on to Kitale, so bags were packed, provisions for the journey procured, plenty of drinking water was taken on board, the vehicle was checked for petrol, water and air, and off they set.

11

The trip to Nairobi

Today cars and buses cover the distance from Mombasa to Nairobi quite easily in five or six hours. In 1948 there was no bitumen surface and the road was pitted with pot holes in some stretches, so that drivers had to pick their way carefully. In those parts where you could travel at reasonable speed the dust was a constant annoyance and hazard.

The first twenty miles were pleasant enough. Climbing up from the coastal strip to the plateau they went through coconut groves and banana plantations. Seisal plants are also cultivated in the area, so they drove through verdant country to begin with. Before too long this gave way to country of a different nature and they came to a region that was quite waterless. The Taru Desert runs for fifty-five miles from Taru to the Taia Hills, and Ernest Gedge left this impression of this crossing in 1892:

> The heat as a rule is intense in these forbidding wastes, the red barren soil reflecting back the glare and heat of the sun like a furnace, whilst the deformed acacia and thorn trees, with their blanched and withered branches, look like so many grim skeletons through which the wind sighs mournfully, seeming to speak to the traveller and to say, "Turn back, for this is surely the valley of the Shadow of Death."

Seven years later Gedge's forebodings were realised when three men in F. J. Jackson's caravan died of thirst while they were making the Taru crossing.

Neville was not worried by lack of water but the dust was a menace. The first overnight stop was at Voi, and just before they set out from there on the second morning a woman was brought in on a stretcher. Two cars travelling in opposite directions could not see one another because of the dust stirred up by cars that had just passed and they collided. The only thing to do if there was a car in front was to drop back far enough for the dust to settle. Even today Voi is the only town of any size between Mombasa and Nairobi, but in those days it boasted just a few shops or dukas and a hotel. The next stage was to be Mac's Inn which they hoped to reach that evening. They started off very slowly because of the dust but after half an hour the situation had improved and they were able to make better speed. They had gone only twenty miles, however, before they came across a lorry at the side of the road. It had broken down, and the man standing alongside told them that he had already sent for help. Vultures were wheeling ominously overhead and the man explained that he had a corpse on board – he was taking the body to Nairobi and had to inform the wife of the deceased of what had happened. The man had died in the bush and so far there had been no means of letting his wife know.

Sobered by the thought of this aspect of Kenyan life, the family travelled on, only to come across another lorry broken down some twenty miles from Mac's Inn. It was about 4.00 p.m. and a man, his wife and two children were all huddled in the cabin. They were terrified of lions and were in fear of what might happen if no one came along. They would certainly have been in trouble if they had had to spend the night there, but when the Allertons arrived at Mac's Inn, Neville arranged for a vehicle to be sent out for them.

THE TRIP TO NAIROBI

Today with people going on safari in Kenya and guides actually seeking out lions and other wild animals for tourists to photograph at close quarters and with little danger involved, it is informative to know the background and to appreciate why these people were so terrified.

12

The man-eaters of Tsavo

Mac's Inn was named after the original owner, Macarthur, but today it is known as Tsavo Inn following its renovation in 1963. Tsavo became well known through the incidents that occurred nearby and the book that was written about them, *The Man Eaters of Tsavo*.

In 1896 a start was made on the East African Railway that was to drive a line from Mombasa, through Kenya into Uganda. Initially progress was good, but trouble struck once they reached the area which now constitutes the Tsavo National Park.

Wild life abounds here even today, but animals were far more prolific at the turn of the century – and lions were amongst these. An adult lion needs something like forty kilos of meat every four or five days. If it kills the equivalent of twenty zebra a year it will survive.

Lions in the prime of life manage this without difficulty when there is plenty of game about, even though only one in five hunts ends in a kill. Ageing lions find it a lot harder and it is sometimes these which turn into man-eaters.

When the railway construction camps were set up attacks on the workers began. Two men were taken from their tents and killed. Panic set in amongst the workers, and eventually they refused to proceed with the work. More than ten lives were lost and with work at a standstill it was critical that the problem be solved.

The Commissioner of Railways Police, C. H. Ryall, happened to be in Mombasa at a time when two Europeans,

75

Parenti and Huebner, wanted to get to Nairobi quickly. The Commissioner agreed to take them by rail as far as the line went, and to get them on to Nairobi if they would help him set a trap for the rogue lion that was causing the trouble. They agreed and accompanied him to Kima.

That evening on the instructions of the Commissioner the carriage that he was in was detached from the rest of the train and shunted to a platform on its own. When everyone else had gone off to sleep the three took turns to keep watch in two hour spells. A. Parenti kept first watch from 11 o'clock and handed over to Ryall at 1.00 a.m. The idea was to try to entice the lion to attack by leaving a light on in the carriage with the door open. The one on guard was sitting opposite the door so that as the lion approached he would have no difficulty shooting it. The plan worked perfectly and between 1.00 and 3.00 a.m. the lion did approach the carriage. It came through the door as expected while the two not on duty were asleep. One was in the top bunk above where Ryall was sitting and the other on the floor under the bottom bunk. But at this point the plan went tragically wrong. Ryall presumably had dozed off and did not see the lion approach. It killed him instantaneously, but as it entered the carriage its weight titled the carriage slightly to one side and the sliding door closed over behind it. The two other men had been woken by the commotion – the one on the floor was pinned down by the weight of the lion on top of him and the one in the top bunk had fallen down in fright and was on top of the lion. For a time it was unable to extricate itself but eventually it managed to scramble out of the window carrying the body. Huebner promptly locked himself in the toilet next door and would not budge from there till light dawned – Parenti meantime ran to the stationmaster's door and beat on it in terror. For quite some time they would not open up, but when they did they learnt of Ryall's fate and immediately telegraphed for help.

A search was mounted first thing in the morning, and the decapitated body was found in the bush nearby. Despite a concerted effort the rogue lion was not caught for another nine months. And it turned out to be a vigorous male still in the prime of life.

When the family came to know of that particular story we do not know, but they had their own excitement at Mac's Inn. The first night they were there they heard loud roaring nearby. A lion had broken into one of the native huts. A few nights before a man-eater had caused trouble, so a group was quickly called together and went after the lion. This time they bagged it quickly and when this one was shot it did turn out to be a very old lion.

Undeterred by the events of the previous day and night, Neville and Olive once again boarded the Land Rover while Jean and Bill clambered into the back to make the trip to Mzima Springs. These are located twenty-six miles from Mac's Inn and are situated in a basin surrounded by low, undulating, conical shaped hills. There is no ground water at all to be seen, all the water going underground and emerging at an oasis of green trees and shrubs that stand out in marked contrast to the surrounding thorn bush standing eight to ten feet high. The red sandy surface on the road gave way to a hard stony base with numerous sharp pointed stones dotting the road. Twenty miles an hour was the most they could do and in places, with plenty of sharp pointed stones, this was cut to five. As they were driving in to the park they saw plenty of game. Gazelle were there in their hundreds; herds of zebras were grazing peacefully too, and giraffes nibbled away at the tops of acacia trees as they drove by.

They had set out very early from Mac's Inn but even so the elephants had finished their morning drink by the time they arrived and were already strolling off, trumpeting loudly. When the springs emerged from underground they were crystal clear and formed a small lake over a hundred yards wide and several hundred yards long. From here a stream ran off carrying the water away to the point where much of it was tapped for Mombasa's water supply. This is a favourite haunt for hippopotamuses, and a number of them were in the water when the family arrived. At one place the water was quite deep – fifteen to twenty feet – but the hippos were quite visible in the water because of its crystalline quality. A small jetty had been constructed in the lake, so Olive and Neville and the children were able to get an excellent view of the whole group and especially of the one which had a baby hippo on its back. The underwater observation tank that has been built at Mzima Springs enables visitors to watch the hippos walk along below the surface. Closing ears and nostrils they move along with huge, slow-motion steps which are surprisingly graceful. In other places people can view hippos as in the Mara River, but there the muddy waters prevent seeing more than the snouts of these huge amphibians as they surface every minute or so while they wallow on hot days to prevent overheating.

The notices that greet visitors at Mzima Springs alert them to the fact that this really is a haunt of game. "You are likely to meet wild animals on this path and the park authorities can accept no responsibility for any eventuality" is the first sign. A hundred yards further on at the edge of the lake appears "Hippo path". Fifty yards past the observation tank the next sign is more ominous: "Do not go near the water's edge. Crocodiles." and then nearby a less ominous one: "Do not feed the monkeys."

After a picnic lunch under a shady tree overlooking the lake they all boarded the Land Rover for the return trip. They were well pleased with themselves – besides the very attractive setting of Mzima Springs and what they had seen there, they had passed a colony of baboons and four rhinoceroses while driving in.

As they were driving back, and before they had come through the stony patch of road, they caught sight of another rhinoceros. Unlike the ones they had seen in the morning, which were well off the road and which paid no heed to them at all, this one was very close – no more than twenty yards from the road.

The rhino had caught their scent, resented their intrusion and was pawing the ground. The road was too narrow to turn the car around and they were in no position to race past it. So they drove on quietly and when they had gone past, the rhino decided to charge. Neville now put his foot down and disregarded any danger of ripping tyres to shreds – but the vehicle gathered speed very slowly and the rhino was gaining on them. It was perilously close, so close that Bill could actually feel the rhino's breath. Fortunately the Land Rover did get up speed and shook the rhino off, but for a few seconds it was touch and go. And it was such a harrowing experience for Jean that she swore she would never go into the Tsavo National Park again.

Years after this incident Abdul Sumra was asked what would have been the best thing to do. At the time he was working as a guide for Wildtrack Safaris and was regularly taking people on safari into the Serengeti. His comment was: "A rhino can run at forty to fifty kilometres per hour. The best thing to do is stop the car, turn the ignition off and sit quietly. The rhino will touch the car with its horn and then move off. But if you accelerate or make a noise, the rhino will charge." Even if Neville had known of that advice at the time, he would have been pardoned for ignoring it and doing exactly what he did.

Back at Mac's Inn they relaxed quietly till the evening meal and then made ready for an early departure the following morning. A herd of wildebeest and gazelle raced across in front of the bungalow while they were sitting quietly on the verandah – doubtless they had been frightened by lion or cheetah on the prowl. During the night wild dogs were heard barking around the settlement but without evident effect.

After breakfast they tied their gear down securely and were again on their way to Nairobi. A feature of the early part of the trip was the view of Mt Kilimanjaro. They were lucky to have struck an exceptionally fine day on their first trip because they got a clear view of the mountain wreathed in snow against a cloudless blue sky. They made the trip many times in the future and were often unable to see it, but on this occasion they had a remarkable view. Like Mt Elgon, under whose shadow they were to live for close on twenty years in Kitale, Kilimanjaro has a long, broad base from which it climbs into the sky. Because it does not rise sheer and stark to a pointed pinnacle it does not give the impression of height that some of the Alps in Europe do, but on a good day it leaves the onlooker with a feeling of awe and wonder, especially when the foreground is occupied by giraffes silhouetted against acacia trees with Kilimanjaro in the background.

From Mac's inn the next item of interest was Makindu Sikh Temple. This was built in 1926 and was further evidence of the sizeable Indian community in Kenya. Refreshments are always available here and hospitality extends to a room for the night for those so inclined.

Between Mombasa and Mtito Andei, which is the district where Mac's Inn was located and the headquarters of the

Tsavo National Park, a feature of the terrain was occasional Baobab Trees. The nearer the coast the more common they were, but they stretched a good hundred miles inland and they excited the curiosity of the children in particular. In girth they are amongst the largest trees in the world and they are certainly some of the oldest. Claims have even been made that they can live up to two thousand years. Because its gaunt branches look like roots the Baobab tree is said to have been planted upside down. It has all sorts of uses — different parts of it are used for food, soap, medicine, glue, fibre, necklaces and cloth. Known also as the Cream of Tartar Tree its seed is surrounded by a pulp which has this taste and from which a drink can be made.

For the last sixty miles of the journey there were no trees of any sort. Savannah plains comprised the run into Nairobi, and on these there were plenty of gazelles and giraffes, with wildebeest equally common. In the few days that it took them to drive from Mombasa to Nairobi the Allerton family had been given a good introduction to what Kenya had to offer them. The next twenty years were to bear this out.

13

Settling in

In Nairobi they stayed at Torr's Hotel opposite the New Stanley. They had one contact there, a man by the name of Penfold, who was the Assistant Commissioner of Police. The first task was to settle Bill into school. Classes were already in session so he was immediately enrolled at The Prince of Wales School as a boarder.

Neville was in the meantime making enquiries about procuring land. Big numbers of people had already come from England under the Soldiers Settlement Schemes and the best land had been taken up. However, Charles Gair, an Englishman in the Colonial Service in Uganda, had acquired land at Kitale on which he intended to retire. He had been a member of the Legislative Assembly and was a Provincial Commissioner in Uganda. Having more land in Kenya than he needed, he agreed to sell nearly a thousand acres to Neville. None of this was under cultivation and there was no house on the property, so it was a question of starting from the very beginning.

The Allertons had arrived in Kitale on a Sunday afternoon while a game of polo was in progress. Jean had finished her schooling in England so she accompanied Neville and Olive and helped pioneer the farm. They stayed one night at the Kitale Hotel and expected to stay rather longer, but Neville met Keith Gebbie the very first day and the two became friendly. Keith's wife and young son were in England at the time, so it was agreed that the family would stay at the Gebbie's place as paying guests while Olive did the housekeeping. This proved a very satisfactory arrangement and they moved in immediately.

Where they lived initially was seven miles from their farm but for a time this was no problem. Before anything could be done land had to be cleared and a dam built. There was no water on the property but their land was sited on a hill and it was relatively easy to construct a dam with a good catchment area. The land was mostly covered with small low bush, and a contractor was employed to bring in a team of oxen and clear away the bush, using the team and chains. Forty acres were cleared first of all and this was put under maize, which could be used for two purposes — to feed the African workers whose staple diet was maize, and also to sell as a cash crop. The idea was to establish a dairy, but time was needed to have pasture sown down and a herd established.

High on the list of priorities was the building of a house, and most of that work was done quite quickly. An African builder was hired, and he assembled a team of workers who made mud bricks on site for the house. Walls went up and a thatched roof was put on in the local style. Within six months the nine-room house, built around a large living room, with a wide verandah, was ready for occupancy except for one thing — the floors. The floors were to be made of concrete and it took a long while to acquire what was necessary. Cement was extremely difficult to come by and the shortage caused by the war continued for several years after hostilities ceased. By keeping his eyes and ears open Neville picked up small quantities here and there, until eventually the floors were laid and the family moved in.

While the house was being built they had moved in with Bob Fripp's family. This was right next to their farm and saved the long trip to and fro each day. It also made much easier the supervision of the building and of the materials being used.

Neville became very friendly with Bob Fripp and this relationship lasted until Bob's death some years later.

14

Farming in Kitale

Parts of Kitale contained some of the most fertile land in Kenya, but this was on the opposite side of the town from where the Allertons were. None the less their land was quite good and they enjoyed a rainfall of forty inches a year on average.

In reasonable time four hundred acres were cleared and a dairy herd procured. One thing that was imperative before introducing a dairy herd was to ensure that the cattle would not fall prey to ticks. A method used to do this was to run a herd of native hump-backed cattle on the land for eighteen months, putting them through a dip of strong arsenical solution every three days. The native cattle pick up the ticks, and as they are immune to most of the local diseases they are like decoys, picking up the ticks which are then killed when the cows are put through the dip.

Such a process takes a long time, involves considerable expense and requires the construction of a dip about sixty-seventy feet long, nine feet deep and two feet wide. It took Neville twelve months to construct his own dip, but in the meantime he put the cattle through the one in the neighbouring property belonging to his friend Bob Fripp. In this way ticks were effectively controlled, but what did wreak havoc on the herd was foot and mouth disease. For two successive years the cattle were affected and heavy losses sustained. The usual precautions were taken — walking through a shallow ditch of water impregnated with disinfectant on entering or leaving the farm — but cows aborted, calves died and milk production plummeted. One whole herd was a virtual write off.

At the height of the most successful period on the farm eighty cows were being milked, but the usual number was closer to forty. The cream was taken from the milk and this was sent into Kitale two or three times a week, depending on the weather and the condition of the roads.

Early on, Jean worked at the Primary School in the town, performing the duties of a matron there, but soon she became interested in raising poultry and gave up the matron's job. Two fowl houses were built, each holding five hundred hens, and next to them a storehouse was put up. This project was going well until one night when Neville was away from the farm – the one and only time that Olive was left alone. During the night a severe storm burst upon them unexpectedly – the continuous rumbling of thunder was ominously close and was accompanied by persistent flashes of forked lightning and lashing rain.

In the midst of all this the Neopara (head man) kept pounding on the door. When Olive got up to find out what the trouble was she saw that the fowl sheds were on fire. They had been struck by lightning and were already a wall of fire – flames were leaping thirty feet into the air despite the falling rain, and in a short time sheds and fowls were no more.

Although the farm supported the family there was never enough money to tide them over a succession of bad years. For fifteen years they carried on clearing the land, planting pasture, putting up farm buildings, erecting fences and doing the countless jobs that pioneering a farm entails.

A number of people in the district planted coffee, and in due course Neville tried his hand at this too. It takes three years for coffee bushes to produce beans so there was no quick return from this venture. No one in the district made an outstanding success of coffee growing, and today there is little evidence of coffee in the district. It did not become a money spinner for the Allertons and they had to rely on the dairy.

One thing that was very successful was the vegetable garden. Olive put one of the Africans, Pedro, in charge of eight men whose job was to tend the garden, and they soon had a wide variety of vegetables flourishing. Cabbage seedlings were one thing which they grew in large numbers, for Olive passed these on to the African women to grow for their own families.

Part of the four hundred acres that had been cleared was sown with maize, a cash crop that brought in some revenue. The African workers were eventually able themselves to provide the maize that they needed for their own consumption, following the custom of allocating an acre or so to each family. Labour was cheap and there was a considerable number of workers on the farm, and with them were their families. It is usual to have about fifty men working on a farm even today – milkers, pit saw workers, fencers, house boys, tractor drivers, gardeners, brickmakers, night watchmen, foremen, maintenance men, lorry driver, dairy clerk, tile maker. If each of these has a wife and even two children (often there will be more) you have a large group associated with each farm.

Locusts and white ants were potential problems, and on one occasion locusts swept in and did considerable damage. Olive was driving back from Kitale with Abok, the head man in the house, when they suddenly came across a swarm of locusts which covered the road to a depth of about three inches. The fields on each side were similarly covered. The car slipped and slithered its way forward, and the number of locusts on the ground was equalled by those in the air. Olive and Abok swathed themselves in cloths to get some protection, and with slits left for their eyes and little else they made their way back to the farm. But the next morning there was devastation everywhere – the locusts had swept through fields, garden, lawns. Every blade of grass had been stripped. The only ones to benefit were the African woman, who gathered quantities of the locusts in tin containers whose contents they later consumed with great relish.

Throughout their time on the farm Neville was regularly unwell. There would often be a day or more, and occasionally even a week, when he was unable to work. This took its toll, and though he supervised work on the farm and worked as hard as any, their financial position grew progressively worse.

15

Aspects of life
peculiar to Africa

Had the Allertons gone to Canada or Australia in 1948 to set up their farm they would have experienced some of the same problems that they encountered in Kitale, but certain features of life there could be encountered only in Africa.

They were in an area that had very heavy concentrations of game right up until farming began and fencing of the land was undertaken. Captain Meinertzhagen marched from Kitale to Nandi Fort in Western Kenya on 7th June 1905, and he kept a tally of the animals he saw: "On the march back from Kitale I counted 124 giraffe, 232 topi, 167 Jackson's haartebeeste, 17 bushbuck, 85 waterbuck, 24 oribi, 4 rhino, 7 warthog, 62 Chapman's zebra, 27 ostrich, 14 kori bustard, and 4 lion in a little over ten miles."

It was only after the Second World War that Europeans moved in to the area in big numbers and farming was carried on extensively. Prior to that Africans had not engaged in agriculture in the region, but since independence they have moved in there in big numbers.

In the late forties and early fifties a few lions were seen near the farm but they were rather uncommon. Giraffes were often seen about six miles away, and Thompson's gazelles grazed in the area. Snakes were part of the scene and normally did not cause too much disruption, but there was an unusual incident on one occasion.

One day Olive noticed on her way back to the house that the grass at one spot had been levelled as though the wheel of a car had driven through it. She alerted the men and six of them went off to investigate. They came across a python 17 feet 3 inches long which they took great delight in killing, because python flesh is considered quite a delicacy by some Africans, reputedly tasting like chicken. Olive was happy for them to have it all themselves – she was not tempted to try the local dish.

Within driving distance of the farm was a pleasant picnic spot on the Suam River, where they occasionally camped overnight. They would provide themselves with meat by shooting a gazelle or something similar, although once when Bill went off with his father to get something for the pot, he came across a ten-foot crocodile, which he shot. But there was never any mention of crocodile steaks having been served up for the next meal.

In the same general area the local people had been troubled by a leopard killing their chickens and attacking their calves, so they asked Neville whether he could track it down and shoot it. A hunting party was organized and three men accompanied Neville and Olive. They camped by a stream for two days and nights, and went out early each morning and evening, but without success. On the third morning Neville and two of the men went off again at 5.00 a.m. In the meantime Olive tried her hand fishing for trout, and the fourth man remained at the camp. He had shot a Thompson's gazelle and was in the process of skinning and cleaning it, and they were going to have the liver from it, together with bacon, for breakfast. Working away some fifteen yards from the tent he heard a loud persistent purring coming from behind, and quickly realized that it was the leopard. He could do little about it for the moment as his rife was in the tent, so without panicking he went on skinning the gazelle, and every now and then cutting off a piece of meat and throwing it in the direction of the leopard. Meanwhile he was inching his way towards the tent and his gun. The leopard was engrossed with the meat that had come its way so easily, and at last there was no difficulty in dropping it with a single shot.

Travelling by car was sometimes hazardous because of the poor quality of the roads. In the dry weather the major difficulty was avoiding the pot holes and negotiating the areas hollowed out by ant-eaters. In the wet season it was a different matter. The brick-red dirt turned into a glutinous mess which gave no purchase to tyres at all. Cars slithered out of control, and the only way to get around was by having chains attached to the tyres. Olive was driving into Kitale one day when the car went off the road, down an embankment and overturned. Olive was badly knocked about but did not lapse into unconsciousness immediately. Staggering to her feet, she clambered up the bank and waved for help to a friend who was passing in the distance. Not realizing her predicament he waved back – and went blithely on. Olive then collapsed at the side of the road and was there for over an hour. A swarm of insects attacked her and ate away part of the flesh in her right breast. A car with eight Africans on board came by, picked Olive up and took her into the hospital, where she fortunately made a complete recovery.

The state of the roads had a good deal to do with the social life that was available to pioneers in the Kitale area. Travelling long distances was not possible, and local clubs sprang up to cater for the eight hundred European families that settled in the Trans-Nzoia district. There were mainly British, Scandinavian and German settlers in this part, with clubs around Kitale at Elgon, Endebess and Cherangani. In Kitale itself the Sports Club catered for hockey and rugby, and the Top Club for older people provided some entertainment. None of these clubs were accessible in the wet season, so the people near Kwanza and Knight's Corner used to visit one another at the weekend. It would be unusual not to have visitors on a Sunday unless the family itself was out visiting. The immediate neighbours were Bob Fripp, Alfred Fripp, Keith Gebbie and Alan Knight. Another family reasonably close was the Kirsops. The husband had lived as a bachelor on the farm after the First World War, and was one of the early men to take advantage of the Soldier Settlement Scheme. After many years as a bachelor he returned from one of his trips to England with a wife. She had been an opera singer, and a fine big room was built in the house where she could give concerts. A grand piano was imported, and Olive and Neville were invited to one of the first performances. Mrs Kirsop was well past her peak as a singer, and Olive never again availed herself of an opportunity to hear her, preferring the bridge evenings which were the usual way of entertaining.

Loneliness was something with which women on farms had to contend. Some coped with this better than others. Those who came to Kenya expecting to have servants do everything for them usually ran into difficulties. Those who involved themselves in an active way did not have to seek out means of entertaining themselves or keeping themselves occupied. Some took refuge in drink, others looked for excitement in extra-marital affairs. These were not isolated incidents, as the question that was current at one stage testifies: "Are you married or do you live in Kenya?" At the same time the extent of such things should not be exaggerated, for that does not do justice to the many wonderful families who pioneered farms in Kenya after the two world wars, and whose lifestyle was the very antithesis of that suggested by one or two recent films on Kenya.

Olive was certainly not at a loss to know what to do with herself. She took a keen interest in people and was in no way inhibited even when she was amongst strangers. She saw that a lot could be done to help African mothers with the feeding of their children and to introduce them to an understanding of the benefits of a balanced diet. She started up a *Mandalayo Ya Wanawake,* that is a Club for Women. She taught the women about protein, what foods would provide this and how to go about procuring these foods, putting her own vegetable garden to good use in this respect. The women were introduced to cabbages and carrots, which were grown from seeds on the farm, seedlings being given to them to grow in their own garden patches.

Other activities included sewing and making patchwork quilts. Olive even taught a group of women a Maypole dance which they put on at the Kitale Show one year, and for which they were awarded a special prize.

Today one might wonder at the wisdom of introducing something so far removed from the local culture, but it was at least evidence of Olive's ability to motivate people and enlist their co-operation. She was a product of her day — had she gone to Africa forty years later she would have been more sensitive to cross-cultural influences.

Mamma Makubwa — Big Mamma — was the name that the Africans had for Olive and attests to the affection they had for her. She was always on the move and rarely relaxed. A favourite saying of hers was "Jump to it". In the evenings Neville liked to listen to music on the wind-up gramophone, and he was an avid reader. Olive came to a liking for reading herself in time, but she was not a natural bookworm like Jean, who would occasionally go off and hide somewhere so that she could have a quiet read undisturbed.

16

The Mau Mau

Within five years of arriving in Kenya, Olive and Neville, like all other Europeans, came to hear of the Mau Mau. Life in Kenya was radically transformed in some areas – in others it went on virtually undisturbed. Around Kitale itself there was no trouble, but at Mt Elgon nearby there were incidents.

The Mau Mau were concentrated in areas populated by the Kikuyu tribe. This covered the highlands and though there were a few individual Kikuyus working in Kitale they were not there in significant numbers. However, the family was affected by the troubles because Bill was drafted into the army as soon as he left school. Everyone turning eighteen was called up and would be engaged in patrolling the forests in groups, two or three Europeans accompanied by three African soldiers. The Mau Mau lived in the forest and emerged to attack isolated farms and terrorize settlers. They were difficult to pin down and their methods struck terror in the hearts of Europeans living on unprotected farms. By threatening to kill them and their families, the guerrillas induced the African workers to take oaths which they felt bound to keep. They could then be told to kill their employers. After a number of such incidents the Europeans did not know which of their workers they could trust. Instances even occurred of servants waiting at table throwing hot soup over the faces of those eating and then killing them with their pangas. During this period Europeans were directed to have a revolver always within reach. Servants bringing food into the dining room were ordered at pistol-point to keep their distance.

Mrs Molly Ryan, an Australian who lived in Molo from 1931 onwards and who survived the Mau Mau period, recounted what happened to a friend of hers, Penny Evans. Kitan was a Kikuyu who had been with the family since Penny was a girl, and he had been working for them until this time. Now he had been ordered to kill her. When he came into the house he told her: "I have been told to kill you, Memsahib." The Evans were from a military stock and Kitan had taken down from the wall a sword that had been hanging there for decorative purposes. He half-heartedly chased her round the house but did not close in on her as he could have done. She ran to the car and found that the keys had been taken. She rushed back to the house to get to the phone and found the wires cut. She eventually got the duplicate keys of the car from the bedroom and drove off to the police, leaving Kitan sitting on the verandah with his head buried in his hands. The police came to the farm and found Kitan's body in a big tank. He had drowned himself.

Kitan found himself in this predicament because the Mau Mau had extremely effective ways of enforcing what they required. Had he refused to do their bidding he would have been tied to a tree and his wife and children cut to pieces before his eyes, and then they would have done the same to him. Presumably he reasoned that by doing what he did he would at least save the lives of his wife and children.

The tension that living in these circumstances created can be imagined. Olive and Neville were not subjected to this themselves, although they did get caught in crossfire when travelling by car to Nairobi on one occasion. They happened to be coming down the escarpment of the Rift Valley when the armed forces made contact with a contingent of the Mau Mau there.

Although massacres did not take place around Kitale, the general unease throughout the country led to numbers of Europeans leaving. Farms were sold up and African farmers began moving in. When independence was granted in 1963 the exodus of white farmers increased, so that today there are now only four expatriate families running farms in the Kitale region.

17

Relations with the Africans

In Kenya there was no segregation of black and white as occurred in South Africa. In the Allerton family the Africans were well treated. They did not receive a high wage but they were well provided for – they received a free house, had land on which to grow maize for their posho, the staple diet, they received gratis all the vegetables they wanted and they had all the wood they needed for cooking. Two years after leaving the farm Olive visited Kitale and met her head man, Abok, in the Kitale Club where he was working as a waiter in the dining room. He was receiving three times as much money as when he had been on the farm, but he was much better off financially when he had been working for the Allertons because of all he received from them in kind.

Olive also had the practice of giving a kitchen allowance. Pilfering was common on some farms – tea and sugar would disappear, and to prevent this pantries were locked up. Olive never did this – the only thing she kept locked up was the liquor. She took the view that it was natural for the workers to want to have a cup of tea when they saw their employers doing this, and she gave them the opportunity to do so without having to steal.

Olive was quite happy for the children to chat to and mix with the African workers, and Bill in particular spent a lot of time with African youngsters. He played with them, learnt to use bows and arrows, was introduced to the art of getting string from trees and making it into traps, and he acquired the technique of trapping birds, rats and hares in the snares.

A few years after settling in Kitale, Olive and Neville began attending the Catholic Church. Soon after, they arranged to have Mass celebrated once a month at their own home, the altar being on the verandah, and those attending gathering on the front lawn. In a black congregation of several hundred they were the only whites.

When they were received into the Church, Neville inscribed their Bible as a memento of the occasion:

> To commemorate 24th February 1956
> A New Beginning for us both. N.C.A. and O.A.

For Olive it was not so much a new beginning as the completion of a journey, whereas for Neville it *was* a new beginning and a rather extraordinary one at that. From earliest childhood Olive had been closely associated with Catholics. Her governesses – Marguerite, Fraülein Schmidt, Mlle Jaggi and Mlle Joska – were all Catholics, and one of them used to take Olive into the church to pray when they were out for a walk until Olive's mother discovered this and put an end to it. The mystique of the nuns in the convent next to Shelley Lodge, her involvement with young Rosencrantz and Francis Chudoba, her years in Vienna and the exposure this gave her to the religious life of the Austrian people – all these things made Olive feel at home in Catholic circles. In Kitale there was a vigorous church life to which she felt drawn more and more. She wanted to be part of the community which gave practical expression to its Christianity, inspired by men like Fathers Prunty and Grennan, and other priests of St Patrick's Missionary Society, the Kiltegan Fathers as they are popularly known.

Neville on the other hand had never been religiously inclined, and when Olive first mentioned her intention of joining the Catholic Church he had exploded: "Over my dead body. I'd rather shoot us both."

This occurred when they were on their way to Kisumu on Lake Victoria. Jean had been married shortly before to Michael Leslie, an Australian who had joined the Kenya police force and was stationed at Kisumu. Jean herself had been in the police force acting as a social worker, and that is how Michael and she had met.

The plan was for Neville and Olive to visit the newly-weds and then take a trip across Lake Victoria for a week or so in one of the steamers that plied the lake.

When Neville responded so vehemently to Olive's disclosure she said no more, but knew in her own mind that she would proceed as she had intended. She resolved to bide her time. They went on the cruise and it was a real delight. Lake Victoria is immense, and some of the boats that carry passengers and goods between the lake towns are of ocean-going size, so a cruise on the lake is for all the world like a sea voyage. Olive and Neville could well have been back in the Mediterranean. For a week they relaxed and enjoyed life on board ship. That gave Neville plenty of opportunity for the reading he enjoyed so much; for Olive it was the chance to meet new people and have the pleasure of a great deal more company than farm life offered.

When they returned to Kitale, Olive quietly prepared herself for the step she intended to take. Meantime, Neville discovered that his best friend, Bob Fripp, who was also their next-door neighbour, had become a Catholic. Bob had become a different man through his contact with an Irishman, the parish priest of Kitale, Father Prunty. Neville became quite aggressive when he learnt of Bob's new-found faith, and stormed up to Father Prunty with the intention of

103

knocking his block off. Father Prunty simply took out a rosary and began praying – and in the face of this Neville crumpled. He also felt the influence of Father Prunty and underwent a change. Religion came to be important in his life, too.

Another priest who played an important part in their lives was Father Tom Grennan. Olive broached him with the possibility of becoming a Catholic, and immediately mentioned that there were likely to be objections from Neville. "I don't think that will be the case", said Father Grennan. "Neville has just been along here to ask me to promise that I will not admit you to the Church for twelve months. That is something I couldn't promise, and one thing led to another and we had quite a long chat. I don't think you'll find him opposed to the idea at all now." And so it proved. Through the combined efforts of Father Prunty and Father Grennan, Neville came round to Olive's way of thinking. He did not end up shooting her as he had threatened; instead he began reading books like *The Faith of Millions* to prepare himself to be received into the Church by Bishop Hoolihan.

Before the date arrived, the Bishop fell and broke a leg. It so happened that Mgr Fulton Sheen was visiting Africa at the time and he performed the ceremony instead. It was just like Olive to end up with one of the best known religious figures of the day, whose broadcasts and TV talks have been beamed all over the world.

On one occasion at a church in Kitale itself Olive had been deeply incensed at the treatment a well dressed African family had received at the hands of the white congregation. When they came in through the main door of the church people in the back pews showed that they were not welcome in their particular pews. This led to their going right down towards the front where Olive and the family were. When Olive became aware of what was going on she made room for them and invited them to join her. She felt deeply ashamed of the indignity that had been inflicted on the visitors.

Colour, race or creed made no difference to Olive. She held strong and deeply felt convictions herself on religion, but she had a tolerance and compassion for people of other races and other beliefs that was refreshing. She really did see them as her brothers and sisters.

She felt that the Europeans in Kenya had some of their compatriots to blame for the trouble that they all experienced from the Mau Mau. The treatment some of the settlers meted out to their black labourers made the resentment of the Kikuyu understandable, though the measures they took to redress the situation were not to be condoned. People who in places like England had never had servants before found themselves in a position to give orders to others, and not all of them handled the situation satisfactorily. Olive herself witnessed labourers being beaten, and she was at pains to treat her workers with dignity and respect, saying "Please — Taffadali" and "Thank you — Asanti".

18

Keeping the wolf from the door

After fifteen years on the farm the prospect of getting comfortably established for life had disappeared. The post-war period when optimism was high was followed by the troubled times of the Mau Mau emergency. Independence came next and many Europeans saw little future for themselves in a country where they imagined they would be regarded as colonial oppressors from the past. Nearly all the ex-patriates around Kitale moved elsewhere.

This alone would not have led to Olive and Neville leaving, but they were in financial difficulty. They had been able to begin the farm with money that had come from several sources. First they had what came from the sale of Artist's Cottage in Findon. Olive's mother left her some money on her death, and Neville's father had given him something to help with the scheme. The balance was procured from the Kenya Land Bank.

A number of ventures had been tried on the farm. Maize was cultivated everywhere and they did grow this successfully. New Zealand flax was supposed to be a good prospect and they tried this but soon had to abandon it. Sunflower was recommended, and tried and also abandoned. The dairy cattle did become established but not without difficulty. Debts had been incurred which could not be wiped off, and eventually the only option left was to sell up and move out.

The next three or four years were difficult ones as Olive tried to find something that would enable her to maintain Neville and herself. Increasingly the burden fell on her as he gradually became less and less able to support them.

She worked in several schools – at Nairobi High she tutored in French and corrected work at a time when Jane Kenyatta was there. She was matron at both Eldoret and Kitale Schools – she spent a year or so at Kitale, and one of the pupils, Jonathan Mayer, who was in primary school at the time, has vivid memories of Olive. She was in the habit of giving the children a hug and he was always afraid of being smothered because at this stage she was a big woman. She was not tall – about 5 feet 7 inches – and she was not as wide as she was tall, but she gave that impression to young children. Jonathan tells of how the youngsters would line up surreptitiously to get a glimpse of Olive and Neville squeezing into their Mini Minor. Neville was also very big at that time and the children marvelled that they ever managed to get in. The school at Kitale catered for children of all religions, and on Sunday Olive would gather the Catholic children and take them off to Mass. When they arrived home she would gather them together and quiz them on the readings from Scripture and what the sermon had been about. She would then explain things that the children had missed. Olive herself was quite popular with the children but this particular exercise did not go down too well with them – it prevented them from being outside enjoying themselves.

On two occasions in the late sixties Neville and Olive were staying at hotels – Bushwhackers and Lake Naivasha – and ended up helping to manage them. Bushwhackers is a game lodge in the region of the Tsavo National Park. One day they were on their way to Mombasa when they saw the sign "Bushwhackers". This was one of the early game lodges and had about twenty rondavels or round huts built in the local style. A fine rock pool was a natural attraction and it was a good place to view wild animals. Several months here was a good initiation into the life they were to lead a few years later at Serengeti.

After they had put in a few weeks' holiday at the Lake Naivasha Hotel they found that the lady managing the place wanted to go off to visit a relative in New Zealand. Knowing that Olive and Neville had already had experience in this kind of thing, she asked whether they would look after the place in her absence. This came at a good time and they readily accepted; for twelve months they lived in the idyllic surroundings of the lake. There were about thirty boats which the guests used for fishing and excursions to Crescent Island in the middle of the lake. Bass and trout were abundant but it was especially telopia that attracted people from far and wide. Many who weren't the fishing type but appreciated a good meal came from afar too, for the fame of telopia had spread by this time. On an ordinary day the water was calm enough, but there were times when the wind whipped up waves which could easily engulf the small boats. A party of French tourists went out one day after Neville had warned them about overloading the boat. Because the lake was dead calm when they set out they paid no heed and took two more people than they should have done. When the wind sprang up they quickly took on water, the boat overturned and they survived only because they were near shore and hung on to the upturned boat until help arrived.

During the Mau Mau emergency Lake Naivasha figured quite prominently, for the reeds growing along the banks in certain places were extensive enough and dense enough to make them good dumping grounds. A number of bodies were found amongst them and murders there were all too common. The wooded areas in the hills near the lake gave good cover and the Mau Mau frequented the region. They got plenty of warning of approaching troops on patrol from the eagles which used the place for nesting. These troubles were all over by the time Olive and Neville came to live there, but the memory of these incidents was still alive. The realization that their son Bill could have been lost in the sort of ambush that was set up in this area made it all very vivid to them.

Bird watching was one of the attractions that drew people to Lake Naivasha. Kenya has an extraordinary variety of birds, and enthusiasts travel there from distant countries nowadays because they can see more species in an area such as Naivasha than they can in the whole of the British Isles. The Secretary of the British Ornithological Society actually stayed at the hotel while they were there. Crested cranes and pelicans are just two of the larger birds that you see in big numbers at the lake. For the hundreds of thousands of flamingoes feeding at the one time or taking flight in dense clouds at Lake Nakuru or Lake Elementeita nearby, a trip by car was all that was necessary. These are soda lakes and produce twenty tons of algae daily, which provides the food supply necessary to sustain such prolific numbers. Films of the flamingoes invariably show close ups of them feeding and then taking flight. What they do not show are the hazards of approaching the flamingoes. Mud flats stretch out a hundred yards or more to the point where there is sufficient water for the birds to feed. Olive had to warn guests to follow only stretches of mud which were quite firm underfoot.

A French woman photographer heard the advice but took little notice. She ended up in a hippo soak and was up to her neck in water and liquid mud before she knew where she was. She managed to save her camera with its telephoto lens only by holding it above her head until she was extricated.

19

Serengeti National Park

Serengeti National Park in Tanzania and the adjoining Masai Mara reserve in Kenya are virtually one complex. Here it is that the greatest concentration of wild animals anywhere in the world takes place twice a year, when over a million beasts migrate. The grasslands in the Serengeti quickly dry out after the long rains in May, and as pasture becomes scarce the animals mass in the south. By some sort of instinctual consensus they all begin to move simultaneously towards the Mara River in the north. Between one and two million wildebeest, zebra, gazelle and antelope set off, and nearly all of them reach the pastures they are seeking. Big numbers of lion, hyena, cheetah, wild dog, jackal and leopard move with them. Stalking prey is not necessary at this stage – they have an abundant food supply ready for the taking and they have easy pickings. Statistically the number of animals they account for is high, but proportionately it is low, and the law of the survival of the fittest works inexorably.

Olive and Neville were offered posts at Seronera, the headquarters of Serengeti National Park, at the end of the sixties. There was an airstrip and a game lodge there which had to be serviced, and they were enlisted to help with these tasks. Although the lodge did not at that point provide accommodation of world class standard – the dining room consisted of a big marquee – tourists from all over the world and from all classes of society were coming to Seronera. Members of royal families, prominent politicians and film stars were common place in the Serengeti as the fame of the place spread and after access was made easy by the introduction of excursion flights by East African Airways in 1957. Prince Philip, Robert Kennedy, James Stewart are typical of the more famous people who came, and the guest book at Seronera reads like a Who's Who of celebrities in all walks of life.

The attraction, of course, was to see animals in their natural habitat and to see them in big numbers. Vehicles would take the visitors to places where herds of elephant or giraffe could be seen grazing. Countless groups of twenty or thirty zebras, similar numbers of Grant's or Thompson's gazelles, dikdiks and wildebeest too numerous to count impress people with the fecundity of nature. In a single day's drive the visitor sees thousands of animals and catches a glimpse of the world as it was in other parts of the globe some hundreds of years ago. Here elemental forces are at work, and the extraordinary change that urbanization and industrialization has made hits home.

Camping out in this situation is an exhilarating experience. It can be done in restricted areas but precautions do have to be taken. The following directions were given to a party on safari in the area where Neville and Olive were:

> Erect your tents in a semi-circle with the entrance facing towards the fire. This will be kept burning throughout the night and another light will be set up on a forty-four gallon drum behind the semi-circle. This is a hurricane lamp. The reason for these arrangements is that a pride of five lions was seen quite near here during the day.
>
> For those wanting to go to the toilet which is fifty yards off near the river let the guard know when you want to go. He will accompany you and keep watch.

And keep watch he did. A Masai warrior wrapped in the blood-red blankets characteristic of their dress accompanied the ladies first of all, keeping his electric torch moving about in constant sweeps over the bush. His spear was at the ready if needed with its metal sharpened shaft at one end. And then it was the men's turn.

Tourists realized that this was not melodramatic posturing when they bedded down for the night and could hear the growling of lions not far away. If proper precautions were taken there was usually no danger.

One party failed to take these precautions during Neville and Olive's time at Seronera. Three young men who had camped in wildlife areas previously and were undisturbed by the proximity of two lions went to bed after supper, let their campfire die down and left no light burning outside their tent. They did not sleep under mosquito nets which would have afforded some protection, and they slept with their heads exposed in the open doorway. Four hours after falling asleep one of the men was attacked. From the spoor marks examined later it is clear that the lion had taken hold of him and leapt twelve feet away from the tent in a single bound. The man's screams woke up his two companions who managed to force the lion to release its grip — it was holding its victim with his head in its jaws. Although he was still alive, his head, shoulder and arm were so badly mauled that he died later that day.

To see a cheetah stalking an animal, people have to go to where that is happening, so tourists would usually be taken in Land Rovers to likely places. Lions can be found sheltering in the shade of bushes or trees, or basking in the sun, but these normally have to be found. They are not so numerous that people just wander out and see prides of lions, in the way that they inevitably see herds of Thomson's gazelles when the season is right.

But there were occasions when the animals came right up to and around the lodge. One evening Olive was at the bar with one of the visitors, talking over the day's events, when one of the African gamekeepers approached her and said quietly: "Memsahib, there is a lion under that tree out there." The lion was between the marquee, in which one sitting of guests was just finishing their meal, and their rooms, and it was a fully mature full-maned lion. Olive told the ranger to go and alert Neville who was on the other side of the bar. He immediately sent for all the Land Rovers that were available, as well as any other vehicles. These were quietly backed up to the marquee and the visitors taken on board. Equally quietly and without any panic they drove around the lion and towards the visitors' rooms. As they did this the drivers switched on their headlights and at this the lion got up and leisurely made its way down the drive — accompanied by the other sixteen lions, lionesses and cubs that were with him!

Giraffes feed off the leaves of umbrella acacia trees and one of these sheltered the room Olive was in. One morning she woke up to find a giraffe feeding off the tree next to the house. It was so close that Olive opened the window, stretched out and patted the giraffe from her bedroom. It ambled off having had its fill, and allowed into the room the sunlight which it had previously been blocking out.

One night a giraffe got itself into some trouble by wandering into the space between two buildings in the compound. It was not aware that an electric cable was strung between the buildings and became tangled up in it. No great harm came of that once the animal was disentangled.

It might have been a different matter on the evening that Olive returned from the lodge to the house they lived in, only to find a huge leopard on the back verandah. The place where the leopard was standing was a confined space, and finding itself hemmed in, it showed signs of feeling threatened. Olive had been told that in these situations the worst thing you can do is show fear. Whether she was conscious of that advice at the precise moment we do not know. She said "Shoo" to the leopard, walked round to the front of the house and left the leopard to make its own way out.

The worst situation that Olive and Neville faced in the Serengeti occurred when they were out in the park late one afternoon. Heavy rain had left low-lying parts quite muddy, and on driving into one of these the Land Rover became hopelessly bogged down. With dark coming on they were in a quandry – should they stay in the vehicle through the night and try to get out the following day, or should they try to walk back? Either alternative was fraught with danger – the Land Rover had only a canvas roof and was not enclosed, offering little protection from marauding animals if any of these resented the intrusion into their territory. Walking out was just as dangerous, especially once dark fell. Olive did not fancy staying with the vehicle, so they set off on foot. There was no immediate danger as the animals at that point were intent on getting to the water holes. Later on would have been the testing time. Fortunately they never discovered exactly how dangerous it was. A light plane flew overhead and they waved and jumped up and down and did all they could to attract attention. The pilot gave no indication of having seen them and flew on, although he had in fact seen them and even recognized who they were. "That is the Allertons down there. They must be in trouble." So he returned to the airstrip, gave the alarm and a vehicle was sent out and picked them up before dark set in.

Olive was a very gregarious person and loved company. Wherever there were people Olive would make herself at home, introduce herself without standing on ceremony, and in no time would be conversing as comfortably as if she had

115

known the person for years. The time at Seronera was full of interest for her, and the constant stream of visitors brought a fascinating cross-section of characters. She would happily have spent the rest of her active life there, but Neville's medical condition put paid to that.

Ever since 1940 and the evacuation from Dunkirk he had been troubled by a duodenal ulcer. One night at Seronera he haemorrhaged badly and Olive found him in a pool of blood when she awoke. A visiting doctor did what he could for him on the spot, and he was rushed off to hospital in Nairobi by plane. Olive had to remain where she was at Seronera for the present, but within a month a replacement was found for her and the need to be close to a doctor and a hospital brought to an end one of the most fascinating periods that Olive and Neville shared in their lives. More adventure lay in store for Olive. But for Neville time was running out.

20
Last days in Kenya

Neville's condition was serious, he was haemorrhaging internally, and was hospitalized for six weeks, although he eventually recovered after a lengthy period of convalescence. It was at this stage that he and Olive discovered Bushwhackers. They were driving from Nairobi to Mombasa, saw a sign on the roadside, "Bushwhackers", and in typical fashion decided to have a look. They liked what they saw, fourteen rondavels serving as accommodation for the guests with a very extensive rock pool with inviting, crystal-clear water. They booked in and were so taken with the place that they remained for three months.

"Bushwhackers" is a private game lodge near the Tsavo National Park. Wild life abounds, with elephants and other animals coming to the rock pool to drink.

The person whom Olive remembers most vividly from Bushwhacker days is Arthur Ashe. She had no idea who he was when she came into the lounge one evening to find him with Tony France. Tony was a professional hunter, and for two weeks Arthur had been going out with him each day. "He nearly came to a sticky end, too", Olive said recalling the incident. "They were charged by a buffalo which emerged from a thicket without any warning. Arthur had one shot and missed, and the buffalo just kept coming. Tony had a bead on the beast but Arthur called out to him: 'Leave him to me.' He took another shot and dropped the buffalo about three yards from him. He needed a lot of nerve to do that. You know, most people talked about what they had bagged during the day when they came in of an evening. But not Arthur. He was a very unassuming person. He had just come from Japan where he was Number One in the tennis world at the time. But you would never have known. He never talked about it."

He did talk with Olive about other things though – books, music, theatre – "the things that so few people talk about in the wilds of Africa" – and she obviously enjoyed his company to have remembered him so well twenty-five years later. "He left a mark on you to meet him. His manners were impeccable and his knowledge of music and literature were surprising considering the fact that he was brought up in such humble circumstances. He did all he could for youngsters, too, because so much had been done for him."

Arthur came back to Bushwhackers while on the same trip, and for a few years they used to write at Christmas time. Olive had a soft spot for Arthur and followed his career with interest.

If it had not been for Neville's condition, he and Olive would have seriously considered going into partnership at Bushwhackers. The style of life appealed to them and the lodge was in a delightful setting. It was not without its hazards though.

One day Olive wandered off to the pool and waded out to one of the little islands a few yards from the bank. On one side the island sloped gently to the water's edge, on the other there was a drop of three or four feet into the water. Olive took her rod out to see if she could land a fish, and was making her way over the well-grassed island to get into a good position for casting. She trod on a log before she reached the edge and the log moved under her feet. In fact it slithered away from her with alarming speed and went into the water with a great splash. Olive had unwittingly trodden on a crocodile. She screamed, dropped her rod and ran for dear life through the water to the bank and back to the rondavels where Neville helped calm her down. "I lost my enthusiasm for fishing at that spot from that moment. It might be all right for Crocodile Dundee, but I know my limitations."

After Neville's discharge from hospital in Nairobi the couple began thinking of setting up home in Australia. Jean and her husband Michael had left Kenya some time previously. Bill had married Gillian Hucks, daughter of an English couple who had come to Kenya immediately after the Second World War. Her father had been in Uganda in the 1920s and had gone out with some trackers after a leopard. One of the trackers took a shot at the leopard and wounded it fatally, but before it died it sprang on Phillip Hucks and mangled him badly, leaving him with a stiff leg and a stiff right hand. He went back to England for medical treatment but was undaunted by the incident. Returning to Africa, he set up a farm in the Cherangani Hills near Kitale and continued going after leopards whenever they attacked his calves. Of such stock was Gill Hucks, whom Bill married in June 1964. When their daughter Jenny was born in 1965 they decided to move to Australia. After Kenya had been granted independence the future for ex-patriates was uncertain, and for the sake of their children Bill and Gill made the break though they both loved Kenya.

With both married children settled in Australia, it was natural for Neville and Olive to think of following them. Neville was sixty-six at the time, and Olive sixty-eight. Following their time at Bushwhackers they arranged for a temporary job at Sun and Sands Hotel at Kikambala, Malindi, north of Mombasa, in the months immediately prior to setting sail. They boarded ship soon after Christmas and arrived in Australia on 26th January 1973. They had to disembark at Portland, the final destination of the cargo ship they were on, and travelled on to Sydney in another cargo vessel. Bill and Gill met them at Sydney and drove them to Rydal, a very small settlement about ten miles outside Lithgow in New South Wales.

They were living on a farm at the time, in a tiny house with two young children, Jenny and Jean. Gill's mother was also staying with them, so when Olive and Neville arrived the house was veritably bursting at the seams. After three weeks at Rydal, Olive and Neville struck out on their own. They headed north to Queensland, looking for something from which they could earn their livelihood. They were hoping for something like a ginger farm or a general store but could find nothing to suit them. They travelled as far as Cairns, and here at last found a property that they felt they could manage. The deal was all but concluded when the lady owner changed her mind and the search was on again.

While resting for two weeks south of Cairns, they saw an advertisement for a general store and post office at Kulpi, a town in the tableland of Queensland. There were a number of things against Kulpi – it was a very cold place set in a windswept valley; it was also remote from clinics, without immediate access to the first-class medical care that Neville's condition required. However, they had to live, so they settled on Kulpi.

The district was a strong Lutheran area, but this made no difference. Olive found the people very friendly and she got on well with everyone. Neville did not have the opportunity to make many friends for he soon fell ill. Besides the haemorrhages he had suffered he was subject to heart trouble, and now he developed cancer. He went into hospital in Brisbane for treatment and was discharged after some time. Bill and one of the girls travelled from Rydal to Kulpi just before Christmas and spent a week with Neville and Olive. No sooner had they got back to Rydal than Neville went into hospital unexpectedly. He had a severe heart attack and died on the night of 31st December 1973.

The whirlwind romance which ended in marriage after Neville and Olive had known each other for only two months had brought about a union which endured for forty years. They faced and overcame many difficulties together; they endured failure together, they learnt to live with one another's failings and shortcomings. But through it all, the love that they came to have for one another in Worthing matured and deepened and carried them through a World War, through pioneering a farm in a distant land, through living in straitened circumstances when financial problems drove them from their home, even through living in hotels and lodges when they had no home of their own.

Fifteen years after Neville's death the love was still there, deep as ever, and fiercely loyal. Those who heard Olive speak of her married life got the impression that Neville was indeed the perfect match, a paragon of virtue. Never once was there the slightest hint that Neville had a fault or a failing. He was her husband, she had chosen to live with him, to support him for better, for worse, in sickness and in health, and she had done just that. When they are reunited on the other side of the grave and the faults and failings of both of them will have been made whole by the Love which was the source of their love, he will be able to take her in his arms again and say

A perfect wife is the joy of her husband.
A good wife is the best of portions reserved for those who fear the Lord. *Ecclesiasticus 26, 2-3.*

Left Olive as a child

Below Olive as a young lady
at Worthing

Olive at the time of her marriage

Olive and Neville

Olive outside a hut with some of her young friends in Madras

Olive in the first wheelchair she used at Beatitudes

Staff and patients at Pope John's Gardens

Leprosy patients at
Pope John's Gardens

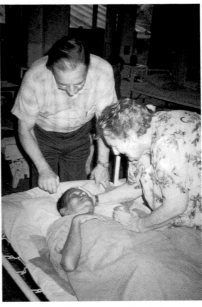

Tending to one of the sick

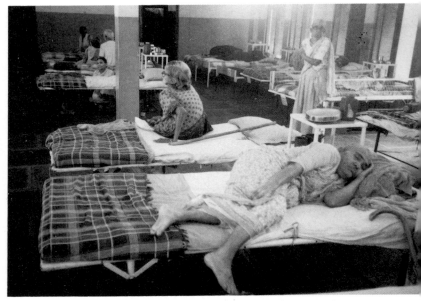

The women's ward in Beatitudes which Olive visited
nearly every day to comfort the patients

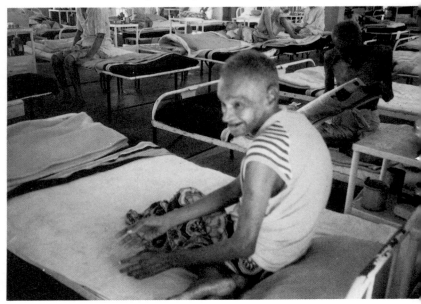

These men would be living in the streets of Madras
were it not for the existence of Beatitudes

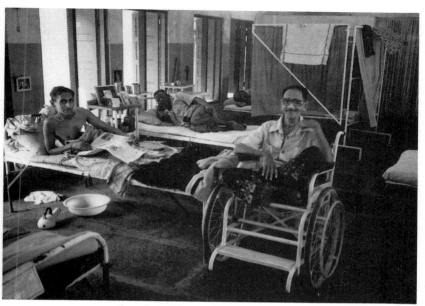

A section of the men's ward in Beatitudes

Olive "loaded" into an Access Cab

The Dominic Savid Boy's Home for the sons of leper parents

Olive at the Lewis Nursing Home in South Australia
five months before her death

21

Post-mistress and storekeeper at Kulpi

Olive was now confronted with the task of running the store and post office on her own. She overheard two of the locals talking together about the situation: "She's bitten off more than she can chew. She'll never make a go of it." If anything was calculated to ensure that she did "make a go of it", that was it. Olive was a determined character, and a challenge brought out her raw courage. Her determination, more than any of her other qualities, enabled her to survive and accomplish things others would not have dreamt of. Her marriage to Neville bore this out; there was so much opposition and disapproval of what they had done from both families that Olive resolved that she absolutely had to make a success of it. Forty years later she was still finding the incentive to see things through because other people doubted her ability to do them. She knew she had the strength to do it, because she knew that she was sustained by God. His presence was the great reality in her life, and she became more and more aware of this as she grew older.

The hours at Kulpi were long. She opened the store six days a week and manned the telephone exchange twenty-four hours a day. It was a small settlement, and boasted a hotel – directly opposite the store – a garage, a Lutheran church, a few houses, and that was it. Farms were scattered about the district, and there were between fifty and sixty telephones which went through Olive's exchange. She was not sitting on a gold mine, but she did make ends meet. There were not too many operas, symphony concerts or ballet performances in Kulpi to match her social life in Vienna, but there was Mrs Reynolds, who had a large property in the district and who had received an education similar to Olive's. She occasionally invited Olive home for dinner, and they were able to discuss things that were of mutual interest. However, Olive did not mind the small talk that was bread and butter for most of her customers. Her interest in people gave her an interest in what was happening to them and their families, and that was the reason for her widespread and ready acceptance by people.

She closed the store on Sundays, and each week drove the seven miles to the nearest Mass centre. After a time she opened up from 8 to 9 a.m. for the convenience of people coming in from outlying farms. She needed to close down for the rest of the day, not only so that she could go to church herself, but she too needed to relax. The effort of keeping things going all on her own left her worn out at the end of each week, especially in the latter years. She was six years at Kulpi, and seventy-five years old when she left, a very active seventy-five, but even so she was slowing down – and she did get tired.

One Sunday afternoon she was taking a siesta between 2 and 3 p.m. when someone appeared at the shop door. The "CLOSED" sign was clearly displayed, so Olive did not respond to the knocking. Then the people moved around to the house door and the knocking continued.

"Come in, come in", said Olive, without stirring from the bed. One of the group followed the sound of her voice and came to her bedroom. When he popped around the corner she saw a mass of flowing hair down to his shoulders and when the rest of him appeared she saw that he was dressed in a black leather suit covered with metal studs and a helmet tucked under one arm. The bikies had come to Kulpi.

"We wanna get some groceries an' some bread."

Olive was too tired to worry about Sunday shoppers.

"Go and help yourselves. Take what you want, write down what you've taken and bring the list to me here. Then we'll work out what it costs."

Taken aback at the trust Olive was putting in them, the twenty-year-old asked, wide-eyed, "D'yer mean yer not gonna come in yerself?"

The bikies gathered up over $100 worth of goods, brought the money in to Olive, and left her to continue her siesta. From then on they came back most Saturdays or early Sunday mornings, but did not disturb her slumbers again.

22

Life in a rest home – "Symesthorpe"

At the age of seventy-five, Olive had retired for the second time. She had found an Anglican Rest Home in Toowoomba, "Symesthorpe", and she moved in there.

Her legs had begun to give her trouble, first the left leg and some months later the right one. These were to get progressively worse as muscular atrophy spread, but for the time being she was still able to get about with the help of crutches. For her age she was remarkably active and she was still as mentally alert as ever.

Life at "Symesthorpe" was pleasant in the extreme. The nursing staff were attentive to every need, care was given solicitously but not overbearingly, a pleasant homely atmosphere existed, and the meals were good. Throughout her life Olive had enjoyed her food, and well into her eighties she was still able to attack a good meal with evident relish. She was not a slave to food, though, and happily ate what the poorest of the poor had when the time came to be with them and share their meals.

Olive was fortunate to be able to drive her own car even at this stage. One thing she liked to do was assist at daily Mass, and the car enabled her to do this. In another part of Toowoomba was the Lourdes Nursing Home, and Olive used to drive over there for the celebration of the Eucharist at 10 each morning. There would be a cup of tea afterwards, then she would hobble back to the car and arrive back at "Symesthorpe" in time for lunch.

On Sundays she would go to the church served by the Blessed Sacrament Fathers, and here she made the acquaintance of Father Ralph Hinton, S.S.S. In the evening of her life Olive's thoughts turned more and more to God, and she began devoting more time to prayer than she had been able to do previously. As she gave herself more explicitly to the spiritual life, she was greatly helped by Father Hinton. He introduced her to different ways of praying, familiarized her with books that he thought would be helpful, and provided a sympathetic ear which enabled Olive to articulate her thoughts on spiritual matters and clarify her relationship with God.

In the meantime, she was taking part in the activities arranged at the Rest Home to keep the old people occupied. Afternoon teas, bridge parties, sing-a-longs, craft work, and all the things that are the stock-in-trade of occupational therapists were provided. Olive was very happy with the home and with the quality of care provided, but she began to get restless. When she saw all those people in the home who were mentally alert but doing nothing better with their minds than playing bridge, she thought it was all wrong. Then she learnt that one of the men was going to one of the State schools and giving talks to the children. "What is good for the gander is good for the goose", decided Olive, and in no time she was doing the same. She went along to a primary school each Wednesday and spent an hour with the children, taking one and sometimes two classes. She tried to teach them something interesting or useful, and had a fund of incidents to draw on from her time in Africa. The children enjoyed it all. Who would not welcome a break from the regular teacher if it gave an opportunity to hear about the Man-Eaters of Tsavo, the Kima Killer, or the Cherangani Leopards?

Olive would have liked to do something for the other residents of the home. "When I saw then mooching around, their lives seemed so arid. I wanted to ginger them up. What could I do to give them a jolt?"

They were not all of the same mind as Olive, and most of them were happy enough to end their days quietly, pottering around the home and occasionally taking the bus into town to make a purchase or two.

Olive used to go every Thursday to visit the patients in St Vincent's hospital, but she still felt she was "rusting away", and became more and more convinced that she should be doing something useful. This was reinforced when she attended a mission conducted by a Redemptorist priest. The mission extended over eight evenings, beginning one Sunday and finishing the next. Every night there were devotions in the church, with the sermon as the centrepiece of each evening's session.

One night the priest referred to the question that Gandhi had once been asked:

"What do you think of Christianity?"

"Well, I'm very impressed with Christ, but not at all with Christians", was his reply.

Olive went home that night and that comment kept racing through her mind: " . . . not at all impressed with Christians." The next day the thought was still with her, and the day after, and the day after that too. It would not go away, and it stirred her to action. She talked about it to Father Hinton. His advice was, "If God wants you to do something, He will make it clear when the time comes."

Well, the time did come, and not long after. Even God must have realized that He did not have too much time to play with if He were going to use a seventy-six-year-old lady. He did not whisper in her ear, He did not send a thunderbolt from heaven, He just appeared to let things happen!

One day soon afterwards, Olive was in the shopping centre of Toowoomba. This is a prosperous country town – it might more properly be called a provincial city – but many people think of it as a country town. Two or three streets account for most of its shops, so when a new Travel Agency opened up everybody came to know of it very quickly, and that included Olive. She saw the Travel Agency, went inside and bought herself a plane ticket to Calcutta.

"I don't know exactly why I bought the plane ticket when I did. All I know is that I wanted to go and help Mother Teresa."

A rash, foolhardy decision taken on the spur of the moment, like a number of other decisions at turning points in Olive's life? Or an inspired action, suggested by the Spirit of the Risen Jesus to whom she had been praying for guidance?

Once she had taken that step things began to move quickly. She settled her affairs, arranged to move out of "Symesthorpe", and packed up. Taking leave of her friends did not take long and she did not have to worry about farewells from the family. She had no next-of-kin in Queensland, so she wrote to Jean and Bill in Adelaide and Rydal respectively, gave the letters to friends to post as she made her way to the airport, and she was on her way.

Four years later Dafne Bidwell interviewed Olive and on the basis of that published an article in the 1984 February issue of *The Australian Women's Weekly*. The first part of that article gives a clue to the reason behind Olive's decision to set off for Calcutta. Dafne first of all quotes Olive, and then goes on to make her own comment:

"I decided to go to India because it was the most difficult thing I could think of." Coming from a young person the words above would have the ring of bravado, but Olive Allerton's tone betrayed something of the anxiety she had felt. She was seventy-seven, on crutches, suffering from a progressive muscular disease that restricted the use of her hands and legs – but "not yet ready for the scrapheap."

23

Calcutta and Delhi

Mother Teresa had left Calcutta the day before Olive arrived, in order to attend the ceremony at which she was presented with the Nobel Peace Prize. Olive never met Mother Teresa in person but she came to know her in spirit through the Missionaries of Charity – Sisters and Brothers – with whom she worked side by side at Nirmal Hriday and Shishu Bhavan in Calcutta, and at the Home for the Dying in Delhi.

There are five different branches of the Missionaries of Charity, all owing their foundation to Mother Teresa. There are the Sisters involved in active work, tending the dying, rearing orphan children, reaching out to the poor and destitute wherever they are to be found.

Corresponding to these are the Brothers who do similar work. Initially founded by Mother Teresa, the Brothers were greatly helped by the inspiration of Brother Andrew, an Australian Jesuit priest who felt God was calling him to throw in his lot with them. He has come to be regarded as the co-founder of the Missionaries of Charity (Brothers).

Then there are Contemplative Sisters and Contemplative Brothers who devote their lives entirely to prayer and the worship of God.

Finally, there is a group of priests who live a community life and carry out pastoral work inspired by the spirit of Mother Teresa.

Olive had been in contact with both the Sisters and the Brothers when she had been working at Nirmal Hriday, the

Home for the Dying at Kaligat. However, when she went to Shishu Bhavan she found only Sisters and their co-workers there, for this was a nursery for three hundred children, all of them orphans. It was situated on Lower Circular Road, not far from the Church of St James, in a building which had belonged to the Congress Party. Indira Gandhi gave it to Mother Teresa so that a home for abandoned infants and babies could be provided. Its black and white marble floor and enamel tiled walls are in marked contrast to the environment from which the babies are rescued, but the building gives good service. Eight hundred people are fed here every morning, from huge cauldrons of rice which are prepared overnight by nine cooks. Other activities designed to help poor girls become established and earn a living are also carried on – typing classes, Indian classical dancing, music, singing and drawing lessons to complement the basic knowledge and skills they acquire at school. These activities are supported by the Mennonite Centre, a Protestant group based in the nearby Entally Market, whose charitable activities are financed by contributions from people abroad living in retirement on an old age pension.

Seventeen sisters and twenty-five lay assistants are needed to keep all these activities going. Volunteers help with the nursing, and doctors come in also on a voluntary basis to check the children and the babies, morning and afternoon.

The upstairs windows of the three-storey building next to the baby home are all shuttered and wired over. Physically and mentally handicapped children are cared for in these wards. There are some distressing sights in this part of Shishu Bhavan, for here are children with all kinds of deformities, and volunteers need special preparation to be able to cope with this. Olive was not exposed to this but had plenty to do with the toddlers in the adjacent building. With three hundred of them to be bathed daily, Olive was set to drying and clothing them.

After a day's work she went back to her hostel, took her meal, chatted with some of the other volunteers for a while, and then settled down for the night.

Another place she visited was Prem Dum (A Thing of Beauty) and this did test her out. This was also a home for physically and mentally retarded children, but this time she was not shielded from unpleasant sights. She was conducted around the home by Sister Barbara, and by the time she had reached the last ward she had had as much as she could take. She knew she was not psychologically and emotionally ready to work in a place like this. At the end she sat down on a green bench in the middle of a ward of young boys. A crippled youngster about six years old was perched on the other end of the seat and he immediately began crawling towards Olive. She discovered that he was deaf, dumb and blind as well as crippled. She put her arms around him and cuddled him as her heart strings grew tauter and tauter and a lump rose in her throat. Then she looked at the floor and saw another youngster, a little older, wriggling towards her on his belly, his deformed body and enlarged head reminding her of a squashed spider. When he reached her and raised himself as high as he could, pulling at Olive's leg, she could take it no more. She reached for her crutches, sped out of the ward – her own description was that she "ran" out – and made for the garden and a bench under a palm tree. She flopped on this, her mind in turmoil and her emotions out of control. All she could think was: "Dear God, why?"

The two months Olive had in Calcutta convinced her that she could do useful work in India. She might not have been ready for Prem Dum but there were plenty of other things she could do. Before taking this on permanently there was

135

one last thing she needed to do. Her brother John was still alive in England. If she was to settle in India permanently – and this was the only way she felt she could be of any use – she should visit him first of all. They had not seen one another for thirty years and there was not likely to be another chance. So Olive took the plane to London and spent several weeks with John. He was comfortably off, having done well for himself, and he could not for the life of him understand what Olive was up to. He did not approve of her idea one scrap. That did not deter Olive, though, and back to India she went, although this time not to Calcutta, but to Delhi. A London doctor had some medicines which he wanted taken to Mother Teresa's home in Delhi, so she agreed to act as courier. Instead of going back to work at Nirmal Hriday in Calcutta she went as directed to the Missionary Sisters of Charity at 12 Commissioner Lane, Old Delhi. This is a compound set amongst houses in an attractive part of the city, and the residence here had been turned into a Babies' Home and Orphanage similar to Shishu Bhavan in Calcutta. A number of sisters lived at the orphanage, and Olive was able to lodge here instead of having to find a room in a hostel. The room was tiny, just big enough to hold a bed, but it was convenient to be able to go with the Sisters each day to the Home for the Dying. This has the same name as the hospice in Calcutta, Nirmal Hriday, but is set in a much more open area than the one next to Kali's temple. It is at 1 Magazine Road, Majoni Kittla, close to the Yamuna River Park and just past the Tibetan Settlement where refugees from the Chinese invasion had established themselves in a dense concentration of huts. There is a spaciousness and an airiness about the buildings of Nirmal Hriday in Delhi, made possible by its being on the outskirts of the city; there is even a country atmosphere about the place.

A convenient way of getting about Old Delhi is by motorized rickshaw, and when Olive was on her own this is the way she travelled. It almost proved her undoing though, and could well have led to her being in the Home for the Dying as a patient rather than as a volunteer. The roads in Old Delhi at that time were full of potholes – unlike the beautifully paved streets of New Delhi, which then as now were extremely well maintained as India's showpiece to the world. The potholes were full of mud and slush from the considerable rain that had fallen, and Olive's leg was gashed against a projecting piece of metal in the rickshaw. It was not a deep or serious wound, only about two inches long, on the back of her leg. Travellers to India are sometimes given the advice, "Treat every scratch as a potentially serious injury." It is a pity Olive had not been alerted to this, for the wound quickly became infected. Olive suspected that the mud thrown up from the potholes was the cause of the trouble, and within two days the leg was up like a balloon. She collapsed in her room and was found there unconscious when she did not turn up for the next meal. The Sisters phoned the Australian embassy, to which she was taken immediately. The staff there arranged for her to be admitted to a nursing home, and for a time it was touch and go whether the leg would have to be amputated. Olive was lucky to be in the hands of a competent Sikh doctor, who saved the leg. For two weeks she was in the nursing home – the name for a hospital in India, as distinct from a home for old people – and she discovered that the Sikh doctor had an Irish wife.

She made a good recovery and was back in action within weeks. She had survived a septic leg and she had survived her first spell in an Indian hospital – on both scores she could count herself lucky.

Olive recounted this incident in a very matter of fact way, as though being faced with losing a leg was common enough, rather like catching cold – nothing to fuss over, just something that happens, and when it has come and gone you simply go on as before.

There was an interruption to her daily routine in Delhi occasioned by a chance meeting with a young man in a "hotel" (a "hotel" in India can mean anything from a five star air-conditioned complex, to a tawdry open air shack with dried coconut palms for a roof). Olive was having a meal of rice and curry in a very crowded, modest "hotel" when Sham Rau sat down alongside her. Olive took the initiative and made conversation with him. When he had overcome his shyness and relaxed after a few minutes he began telling Olive what his work involved. He was a very poor, very humble young man, living with his wife and family and mother-in-law in a village between Delhi and Agra. The plight of his people worried him greatly, to the point where he involved himself with their problems and realized the need for some training in social welfare. Through the church he was associated with he was given the responsibility of acting as medical aide to neighbouring villages. He was paid ten rupees a day (8 rupees = $1 Australian; 13 rupees = $1 US) to visit families in their homes and bring them rudimentary first aid. Donations of medicine and bandages were received from overseas, and he distributed these throughout the villages to those in need. When he saw how interested Olive was he asked whether she would like to come and stay with his family and find out what village life was like.

Olive never missed an opportunity like this, and within days she had joined Sham Rau and his family. She lived just as they did, had the same food, slept on the floor, drank the same water. Water is a source of endless problems for

138

Westerners in India, and a great deal of trouble is taken to sterilize drinking water by boiling it for half an hour, putting it through purifiers or treating it with tablets like Puritab. "Delhi Belly" is one of the colloquialisms for diarrhoea and allied complaints that afflict people whose systems cannot cope, and it strikes a high proportion of visitors. "When away from home, never drink water, and eat only those foods that nature has given some protection to." This is quite restrictive, but for newcomers it is a good rule of thumb to go by. Tea or coffee are reasonably safe, bananas, apples, mandarins, sweet limes (very similar to our oranges) are readily available and will keep a traveller going until he gets to a "safe" place to eat and drink. That way of acting is acceptable when a person is travelling, but in Olive's case she judged it better to have exactly what the family had. She experienced no ill-effects from the water but found the food difficult to get used to. Breakfast consisted of some rice water, with the one real meal of the day in the evening. This was a plateful of rice helped down with dahl (which resembles thick lentil soup) and vegetables. For the first week Olive was constantly hungry; after this she became more accustomed to the regime and was not so conscious of pangs of hunger. Beds were non-existent, a mat on the floor doing service for a mattress. This would be rolled up during the day to give more space to move about, for the house had only two rooms, with an outdoor kitchen. There was no toilet. Olive had to steel herself to follow the local custom which was to use a clump of bushes near the river as a latrine – men to the right, women to the left. Probably nothing is more difficult for Westerners to come to terms with in India than the custom of people relieving themselves anywhere and everywhere. The sight and stench that this causes in some places is revolting and takes some getting used to. For Olive this was further complicated while living with Sham Rau's family by the children of the village. A white woman living in their very own village was quite an oddity, and they followed her to the bushes to see if she was white all over!

The month she spent in the village was the most difficult she had in India, but she treasured it for the understanding it gave her of the people and for the empathy it established between her and them. She discovered that there was a great deal of happiness in these families, in spite of their poverty. Their willingness to share whatever they had was an eye-opener. What they had might be a miserable pittance, but they joyfully observed the rules of hospitality to give generously of that pittance to a guest.

She came in contact with the Harijans at this time and learnt that caste is still a potent force in Indian society. Gandhi did a great deal to improve the lot of the Untouchables, those outside the four classes into which people fall: (1) Brahmins – priests; (2) Kshatriyas – administrators and soldiers; (3) Vaisyas – artisans and merchants; (4) Sudras – farmers and peasants. Harijan, Child of God, was the new term Gandhi coined for the Untouchables. Laws were passed which were designed to allow them to take their place in society, but legislation did not eliminate discrimination, and Olive saw evidence that the Harijans were still "untouchable" in the eyes of many people. In the very year she arrived in India, 1980, a number of Harijans were killed when a riot broke out, caused by a bridegroom not dismounting from his wedding horse when passing a group of higher caste men! When the shadow of a Harijan walking by passed over the food of two workmen sitting on the ground eating their lunch, they immediately threw the food away – it had, in their eyes, been contaminated! In the village of Sham Rau the Harijans were not permitted to draw water from the well; someone else had to bring it up for them because if they did it no one else would be able to use the well again.

Olive was distressed by this kind of thing – it went against all her deepest instincts and was contrary to her own practice in Africa. It made her conscious of the deep pain experienced by people rejected by other human beings and she was soon to have an opportunity to redress this in some small way.

She remained nearly a month with Sham Rau and then returned to Delhi. Her time here was coming to an end too. Altogether she was three months in Delhi and then moved to Madras. For some reason she wanted to go to the south of India, so it was arranged with the Sisters there and in due course she made the move. There was no room in the actual convent, but at the children's home two hundred yards away there was a room attached to the clinic. Olive was satisfied with this accommodation and spent her time assisting the children. The Provincial of the Missionaries of Charity for the South of India was based in Madras, and when she visited the community was very concerned at the conditions Olive was living under. A semi-invalid of her age should have much more comfort than that, she thought, and very quickly arranged with a woman doctor for Olive to stay with her in her home. Olive spent one night there, but instinctively felt it was all wrong. If she had come to help the poor she should be with them and not allow herself to be pampered in upper-class surroundings.

In characteristic fashion she took action immediately. After breakfast she asked for a rickshaw and when it came along she told the driver: "Don Bosco's". She had heard that there was an institution of that name for destitute people somewhere in Madras, but she did not know that the Salesians had seventeen institutions in the city of Madras alone. The Salesians are a religious congregation founded

by a priest, John Bosco (1815-1888) on the basis of the
spirituality of St Francis de Sales. This gave rise to the name
"Salesians." They are a remarkable group and have had an
extraordinary growth, now numbering eighteen thousand
men, with priests and brothers in virtually every country of
the world. There is a corresponding number of Sisters who
are equally widespread.

Their special work is with youth and embraces projects
such as schools, summer camps, youth hostels, orphanages,
technical institutions and homes for the handicapped and
for delinquents. The gentleness of St Francis de Sales – "You
catch more flies with one spoonful of honey than with a
barrel full of vinegar" – found expression in Don Bosco's
belief that persuasion is more effective than punishment. In
the nineteenth century, when stern discipline was common,
he pioneered the "preventive system" of education. As a
result the fatherly love of Don Bosco has become a characteristic of his spiritual sons and daughters. A family atmosphere is the hallmark of Salesian institutions the world
over, and numerous people who themselves have been
involved in working with young people have marvelled at
how close the Salesians are to their boys and girls.

In India they have two hundred and fifteen communities
and institutions grouped around six administrative centres
– Bombay, Calcutta, Guwahati, Dimapur, Bangalore and
Madras. The region administered from Madras takes in Sri
Lanka as well as the state of Tamil Nadu, but it was in the
Tamil capital of Madras that Olive found herself asking the
rickshaw driver to take her to Don Bosco's. Fortunately, of
the seventeen Salesian houses to which the driver might
have taken her, the one where she ended up was ideally
suited to her purpose, for he took her directly to Vyasarpady, a slum area on the outskirts of the city. Here was
"Beatitudes", a home for destitute people of all sorts, young

and old, physically and mentally handicapped, babies and young women, orphans and children from leper families.

Olive asked for the priest in charge and was introduced to an Indian, Father Ittyachen Manjil. She explained that she had come from Australia in order to help in whatever way she could, and asked if she might stay at "Beatitudes". Father Ittyachen was scheduled to leave for Bangkok within a matter of hours to attend a conference there on "The Educational Methods of St John Bosco". He told Olive that she would be welcome to stay for the two weeks or more that he would be away, and that she might be able to find something useful she could do in his absence.

Olive was initially given a makeshift room which was adequate, but little more. Accommodation at that point was at a premium, and in time when another building was put up she was given a more satisfactory room on the ground floor. At any given time there may be half a dozen volunteers at "Beatitudes". Quite good rooms are provided for these on the first floor of the main building, but Olive's difficulty in negotiating stairs made it desirable to house her at ground level.

The basic nature of the accommodation can be gauged from the fact that one night Olive was awakened by a large rat scurrying across her face. What feelings this gave rise to can be imagined, and even more the sensation she must have had the following night trying to compose herself for sleep. "Will it come back again tonight? What if it bites me? Will I contract some horrifying disease?" Her equanimity was undisturbed, however, and as with every other difficulty she just laughed about it afterwards. It is almost as though God had spoken to her, as he had spoken to Joshua thousands of years before, and given her a composure which she preserved in very trying circumstances: "I will always be with you. I will never abandon you" (Joshua 1:5). She later described this sense of God's protective care always being with her when she said that she felt that she was like the abalone divers who went down into the sea in a protective cage. They were able to go about collecting abalone undeterred by the possibility of sharks coming around. In the same way she was able to go about her business, confident that God always had her in His hand.

24

"Beatitudes"

Once Olive had settled in, she went on a tour of inspection. The grounds are quite extensive, covering about fifteen acres. "Beatitudes" was quite deliberately sited in a slum area so as to bring succour to people where they needed it most. That inevitably meant that the area was *not* in a suburb that was highly prized as real estate. In fact, the home was built on wasteland to the north of the city near Cochrane Basin Road and Buckingham Canal. A plant for generating electricity had been built in the area, but it was of such poor design that it poured out tons of ash into the atmosphere every day, much of which was deposited in Vyasarpady. Olive commented on everything being covered with coal dust every day, no matter how faithfully the rooms were dusted. About two years ago the plant was closed down because it was such a health hazard and so many people in the district had come down with lung complaints. While Olive was there it was still going full blast and gave her an additional reason for a daily shower.

Her tour of inspection took her first to the infants' section. Several classes were being conducted by Indian women in their saris, which did wonders to brighten the surroundings. About two hundred boys and girls up to third grade were being taught in rooms directly opposite the main building. At the end of the infant section was a small room where six toddlers were being cared for. Olive's heart went out to these babies, for they had just been brought in from the streets where they had been abandoned. They were being treated for malnutrition by two nursing aides, who were feeding them at that particular moment with glucose solution. As soon as they had been brought back to normal they would be placed in the nursery with the other youngsters.

Next to the infant school was a big room with sewing machines and fifteen girls being taught dressmaking. They proudly showed Olive the patterns they had made, and she admired the albums with samples of the exercises they had done.

The next call was to the wards for the old people. Beds for forty-five men and forty-five women were provided. When the inmates arrived they were usually at death's door. Within weeks they would normally be back on their feet, and some of them lived on for another twenty years.

The old people's section brought Olive to the end of the compound. An elderly man in military uniform was on guard in his sentry box at the gate, and Olive wondered how it was that the Indian army was involved in these activities. She later learned that the man was in fact employed as a security guard and merely looked like a member of the armed forces. An open drain full of refuse of all sorts was on the side of the road between the main compound and the school attached to "Beatitudes". She picked her way safely over this and then stepped down into the school yard. "Beggars can't be choosers" was too obviously true in this case. These were virtually beggar children and the only location for their school had been here, in a plot six to nine inches lower than the surrounding roads. The inevitable result is that whenever it rains the school yard fills with water which seeps into classrooms, and lessons have to be abandoned. It had not been uncommon for periods of two or three weeks of schooling to be lost at a time.

Retracing her steps, Olive came back into the main compound and was taken into the kitchen area. There was access to one part of this from outside the compound, where between eight hundred and a thousand people were fed with rice every day. The huge vats which Olive had seen at Shishu Bhavan in Calcutta had numerous brothers and sisters here, and generous helpings were ladled out between the hours of twelve and 1.30 p.m. every day. "The cost of maintaining 'Beatitudes' must be enormous", thought Olive. "How is it all financed?"

Dining room, dormitory block and administration section rounded off the rest of the main building. All that remained were the workshops for metalwork and woodwork and another dormitory block. Olive was surprised to learn that there were a number of lepers at "Beatitudes", and that the workshops had been specially provided to cater for their needs. In Southern India, leprosy is still common and those afflicted with it experience the same rejection today that it has occasioned for thousands of years. The belief that leprosy has been exterminated is not correct – in a few of the states adjacent to or near Tamil Nadu (formerly known as Madras State) leprosy is relatively common. Earning a livelihood becomes problematic once a person is known to have contracted leprosy, so the woodwork and metalwork projects were initiated at "Beatitudes" to enable the patients to build objects which could then be sold on their behalf. The number of patients on site was relatively small, for most of them were living some seven kilometres further out at Pope John's Garden. There were, however, some forty or fifty boys and a comparable number of girls living at "Beatitudes", the children of leper parents. The custom in those days was to leave the children with the parents only until they were six years old. It was felt that to leave them any longer with the parents would be to expose them unnecessarily to leprosy.

The last place Olive visited was the dormitory block on the far side of the compound for the children of leper families. Little did she know what that particular building would involve her in.

Having inspected the whole property, Olive now knew what "Beatitudes" embraced. The wide variety of people being cared for in different parts of the establishment gave her plenty of scope. In the absence of Father Ittyachen, Olive was able to work in with Sister Nancy Pereira, an Indian nun who was a member of the Daughters of Mary Help of Christians, the official title of the Salesian Sisters. Sister Nancy had been at "Beatitudes" from the time it began in 1970 until 1974, and then again from 1980 until 1986. Her second spell there overlapped the whole of Olive's period – she arrived there in 1981 and left at the beginning of 1985.

The Madras phase of Olive's life marks its climax. Coming to the end of her days, and having retired twice, it could be expected that she would slip quietly into eternity when the time came. Not so Olive! It was almost as though she had been given a new lease of life. With the responsibility of raising her own family behind her, and now that death had robbed her of her beloved Neville and the need to care and provide for him, it was almost as though there was now nothing to restrain her youthful adventurous spirit from reasserting itself. "Beatitudes" offered her the scope she was looking for.

First of all she started with the tiny tots. Sister Lucy arranged for her to help with these, and there was a great deal of satisfaction seeing life surge back into their little bodies as nourishing food found its way into their blood-streams. She lavished on these babies deprived of their mothers the love which they so sorely needed, and she was amply rewarded by seeing them take a firm hold on life. Before long, consideration was given to making Olive responsible for the crèche, but this did not prove practical. As a foreigner who had been in the country only a matter of months, Olive needed to get to know the Indian way of doing things. The cultural differences are so great and ways of approaching things are so different that this can give rise to problems for people in an administrative position. Olive did experience some difficulty in adapting to Indian ways. Some of the Indians likewise found Olive's ways hard to take. She had always been accustomed to having things done when and as she wanted them done. For a time it was incomprehensible to her that there could be any other way. Her manner could be imperious at times and this was doubly damaging if she was not aware of this, as sometimes happened. She had a tendency to tell people what she intended to do when it would have been more appropriate to ask them. At one point this brought her into conflict with some of the people at "Beatitudes", and until they came to see eye to eye there was some tension. Once this was settled and there was an understanding of what she could do, there was no looking back.

When Father Ittyachen returned from Bangalore he came to know and appreciate Olive. A wonderfully genial character, he had been placed in charge of "Beatitudes" on 24th May 1981. He was the first native-born Indian to be responsible for the administration, and taking over from Europeans was not without difficulty. Dutch and Italian priests had been running the place until 1981, and through their contacts in Europe they had been able to assure a steady flow of finance. This money supply dried up when indigenous people were put in charge. To make matters worse, Government departments now began insisting that

"Beatitudes" should pay levies which had never been required in the past. It was important to put "Beatitudes" on a different financial footing. From being the brainchild of foreign missioners, the venture was to be Indianized and Father Ittyachen was given this task. He set about convincing the Government that it had a responsibility towards the people in "Beatitudes". For some time officials were reluctant to admit this, but eventually they came to accept a measure of responsibility.

It was at this time that Olive began putting some of her thoughts and prayers on to paper and she gradually built up quite a collection. She had a facility for expressing herself, and some of her prayers display a vivid awareness of the sense of God's presence. As she went through life this consciousness of God being present to her and of her being present to God deepened. Even as a child she was drawn to religious things, and as she grew older she intuitively reached out to God and mixed with people who brought her progressively closer to Him.

Olive's great strength was not business acumen or running a section of a big institution — it was her ability to reach out to people in need, to relate to them and to enable them to experience the warmth of her love. They soon discovered that she was not simply "practising charity" or "doing good works" — they sensed the genuineness of her love and they responded to it.

Father Ittyachen has pointed out that Olive's greatest contribution was her very presence. She had been a grandmother for over fifteen years before coming to India, now she became the grandmother figure for the whole of "Beatitudes". Twice a day she would get someone to push her wheelchair over to the wards for the old people, and there she would chat away and pass the time of day, bringing news from other sections of the place and enquiring about the welfare of each one. Because she was not tied down to any one section she became a kind of interdepartmental figure. Sister Lucy was assisted by four other nuns and they each worked in particular areas. Olive roved from one part to another, and because she did not have specific tasks which she had to complete in a set period she had time to give to people.

Sujatha was one of the girls being cared for in the home who benefited from her concern. She had a weak heart and was confined to a wheelchair. Olive took a special interest in her, and from talking to her learnt that she had a brother who was also a cripple. At the time Sujatha was about thirteen and her brother a year or so younger. They had lost contact when Sujatha had been brought to "Beatitudes". Unbeknown to one another, the brother had been brought to "Beatitudes" too, and was being cared for on the same property but in a different section. From going on her rounds and talking to each of them, Olive realized that they must be brother and sister and arranged for them to be brought together. What a reunion it was – they chattered away for hours in their own language, something Olive did not recognize. It was not Tamil, the language of Tamil Nadu, and it certainly was not English, but whatever it was Olive could recognize the immense joy the two were experiencing. It is difficult for us to realize why the two would not have been identified as brother and sister from their names. Olive's children, Jean Allerton and Bill Allerton, would easily have been recognized as members of the same family if they had been orphaned as children and taken to an institution. That does not follow for families in the south of India, though. Naming customs differ and children in some places are given the name of the locality they are born in. As a result, a child's second name might be quite different from the father's second name. Surnames as we known them are not always shared by members of the same family.

Of all the people at "Beatitudes", the one who became most attached to Olive was a Burmese refugee, Lily. A large number of refugees from Burma had settled in Madras, and the tiny businesses they set up in box-like cabinets on the footpaths of North Beach Road near Parry's Corner quickly became known as the Burma Bazaar. It was from this group that Lily came when she procured a job as a cleaner at "Beatitudes" to support her three children. She had been there some time when Olive arrived on the scene, but they did not immediately make contact. Initially Olive was still able to get about on her crutches, but within months the muscular dystrophy had progressed to the point that she was confined to a wheelchair. At this stage Father Ittyachen asked Lily to give Olive whatever help she needed. She soon proved invaluable, keeping Olive's room clean, washing her clothes, and doing the hundred and one things an invalid needs to have attended to. She was sixty years of age, had three daughters, one of whom was retarded, and a son dying of TB. She spent herself for her children, using all the money she earned to maintain them in the absence of her husband, who had previously deserted her. The retarded daughter had to go to hospital by taxi to receive treatment several times a week and this virtually paupered Lily. So as to help feed her children, she would not eat the rice she was given for her midday meal at "Beatitudes". She had two or three mouthfuls herself, then carefully put the rest aside to take home for them. She could not afford the bus fare of forty paise (five cents) each way, and so used to walk the three miles to and from home until Olive discovered what she was doing and rectified the matter. Before this happened though, Lily collapsed one day in Olive's room — it was simply a case of malnutrition. She had been getting a reasonable wage at "Beatitudes", and since a good midday meal was always provided, people were surprised at Lily's condition, and puzzled to know what had brought her to the point of collapse. Then it all came out and Lily, who had been so concerned to help others, now began to receive some adequate help herself.

Olive came to appreciate how selfless Lily was on the occasion of a torrential downpour that engulfed Madras. Seven inches in twenty-four hours was more than the city's stormwater drains could cope with. Lily's own home of coconut branches and rushes was blown in and left a shambles, but her first thought was for Olive. She hurried to "Beatitudes" and found water pouring into Olive's room in one corner through the drain that carried off the shower water. Olive was stranded in her bed and was relieved when Lily turned up. She was in no immediate danger, but it had been somewhat inconvenient.

Olive was hospitalized twice while in Madras, and once lapsed into unconsciousness. Lily visited her every day in hospital and kept vigil by her bedside when she was in a coma. Lily had come to love Olive like a daughter, and she in fact carried out in Madras the role that Jean was to play in Adelaide several years later. Olive came to regard Lily as a saint and marvelled at the way she poured herself out for others. Small wonder that the one person Olive was keen for an Australian visitor to "Beatitudes" to meet on her behalf in 1987 was Lily.

Jesudas is another person from "Beatitudes" who came to mean something special to Olive. The name Jesudas means Servant of Jesus, and like Christodas, is not uncommon. One of the things Olive used to do some evenings was to give tuition in English to young men and women. Though efforts are being made to establish Hindi as the official language for the whole of India, there is considerable, even violent, opposition to this in the south of India where the Dravidian languages – Tamil, Telugu, Karada and Malyalam – are spoken. English is still very much in demand and is a passport to advancement in certain positions. Jesudas was a young man of nineteen, going on for twenty, who had returned to "Beatitudes" during his holidays, and he wanted to improve his English. He went along to Olive the first evening he was back, only to find she was too exhausted to help him that night. The climate in Madras is very enervating for a good part of the year – the months from November to January have mild temperatures. By February the thermometer can be climbing well into the thirties, and from March on the climate can become unbearable, with extreme heat and high humidity. Olive coped well with the trying conditions, but like everyone else she tired and wilted with the onset of the hot season. Jesudas was very despondent on this particular occasion, so in order not to disappoint him too much she suggested that he go off and write up the story of his family and bring it to her for correction the next day. He did this, and what he brought back wrung her to the heart. Jesudas had a sister and an elder brother, and when the time came for the sister to be married there was the problem of the dowry and the payment of the wedding reception. The father did what so many Indian parents do in this situation – he borrowed two thousand rupees (approximately $250 Australian) in return for the elder brother contracting himself as a bonded labourer. This is a euphemistic way of saying that he sold himself into slavery. Jesudas had been a baby of three or four at the time; for the last sixteen years his brother had been working seven days a week from 4 a.m. to 9 p.m. as a farm labourer. The bank manager who arranged the loan had "sold" him virtually to his present "employer". He had run away once and made his way to Bombay, but he was traced there, apprehended and brought back to Madras to work out his bond. The amount of money was such that the family would never be able to pay it back. He was condemned to a lifetime of servitude.

Olive was quick to appraise the situation. She knew that if the money was available the bond could be redeemed and the labourer bought out. She told Jesudas to come back the following day and that she would have the money for him. When he returned twenty-four hours later she had arranged for the money to be drawn from her account and it was waiting for him. Before sending him off with it she had Father Tarcisius explain to him what to do (Father Tarcisius Ratnaswamy had by this time taken over from Father Ittyachen as Director of "Beatitudes"). Jesudas was instructed not to hand the money over to the farmer without witnesses; he was urged to go to the priest stationed nearest the village where his brother was working and ask him to carry out the negotiations. Jesudas went off immediately. The only things his brother possessed at that time were the clothes he stood up in, a loincloth and a covering for his head. The transaction took several days to complete — the farmer disputed the money that should be paid to him, and he was loath to lose the cheap labour from which he had benefited for the past sixteen years. However, there was nothing he could do, since the money was there in ready cash before him, with the priest standing at the side of Jesudas to see that justice was done. It took Jesudas a day to travel to and from the village, so it was about five days after Olive had given him the money that he turned up at "Beatitudes". One day at about 7.15 a.m. there was a knock at Olive's door and when she called out "Come in", Jesudas entered, accompanied by his brother. Before she knew it Jesudas's brother was down on his knees, kissing her feet, and he was saying to Jesudas, "She is like an angel".

Bonded labourers are not uncommon in India; the number of men and women in bonded labour has been given as two million. The Social Welfare Department in the Teacher Training Institute of Sacred Heart College at Tirupattur where Father Ittyachen is presently rector has a programme designed to sensitize people in the region to the problem, and to work towards its eradication. This can be a dangerous undertaking because it threatens the continued existence of a cheap source of labour for some employers who are not likely to take things lying down. Reprisals in one form or another are a possibility.

A weekly occurrence at "Beatitudes" highlights the varying backgrounds of the people amongst whom the Don Bosco Social Welfare Rehabilitation Centre of Madras carries out its work. Each Wednesday morning a motorized rickshaw goes from "Beatitudes" to the Co-Cathedral in the heart of the city. Two hundred yards from Parry's Corner, which is one of the best-known landmarks in Madras, there is to be found Armenian Street, which derives its name from the Armenian Church to which people can still gain access, but which is in fact deserted. A hundred yards down Armenian Street is the Co-Cathedral, so named because there used to be two dioceses in the Madras region which have now been amalgamated into one. The two cathedrals still continue to function as churches, San Thome Cathedral several miles south of Parry's Corner where the relics of St Thomas the Apostle are venerated, and St Mary's in the city proper, now known as the Co-Cathedral. Masses and devotions are carried out here, just as in any other Catholic church in the world, but on Tuesdays something different happens. On that day every week devotions are held in honour of St Anthony and the Child Jesus. A queue forms and at any given moment from 7 a.m. until 7 p.m. five hundred to a thousand people will be lined up in the churchyard waiting to file past the statue, and to make an offering of bread or a roll or other food and possibly money that will then be distributed to the poor. Every Tuesday a crowd of thirty thousand people visits the church, and apart from those who attend Mass early in the morning the vast majority of those who come are Hindus. They adopt St Mary's for the day, and the offerings they leave for the poor are collected on Wednesday morning and given to the needy, some of it going to "Beatitudes". The motorized rickshaw brings back two sackfuls of loaves and rolls which help make up lunch on Wednesday for those coming in from Vyasarpady. Because of the huge number of people who come to the Co-Cathedral every Tuesday, a great number of beggars line Armenian Street from the corner of Netaji Subhash Bose Road to the church. Between a hundred and two hundred of these spend the day there gathering alms, mixed in with street vendors who sell fruit, drinks, sweet-meats, coconuts, flowers and trinkets. A significant propor-tion of these beggars have leprosy, and people giving them alms find themselves putting money into fingerless hands or reaching down to men or women with all kinds of defor-mities. Government institutions exist to cater for them, and efforts are made to encourage people to come forward for treatment. For many this would mean being totally cut off from family and friends, not because the treatment requires this, but because of prevailing attitudes in the community. Olive gradually became more and more involved with these people and spent an increasing amount of time with them. That took her out to Pope John's Garden, and this came to be a place to which she loved go to.

25

Pope John's garden

Olive had not even heard of the religious congregation of the Salesians – priests, brothers and sisters – until she went to Madras, but they were to play an important part in her life from them on. One of them, Father Mantovani, was born in Italy in 1911 and died in India in 1967, so she never had the opportunity to meet him, but the work which he began just before his death touched her very deeply.

For a time Father Mantovani was Novice Master responsible for training young men aspiring to join the Salesian congregation in the south of India. Father Tarcisius Ratnaswamy, currently director of "Beatitudes", was one of his novices and remembers how zealous he was for the dying. In 1952 Mother Teresa had begun gathering men and women off the streets of Calcutta and easing their last days in Nirmal Hriday. Father Mantovani did the same in Madras, but his home for the dying was in "Beatitudes". Some of those Father Mantovani came in contact with were not at death's door, but as leprosy patients they might just as well have been. In many families, as soon as a person was known to have leprosy the others wanted to have nothing further to do with him. Father Mantovani found a temporary home for these people at "Beatitudes", and was soon planning a special home for them outside the city altogether. Vyasarpady was not an attractive district, and Father Mantovani wanted to provide an environment for these stricken patients which would be pleasant and cheerful. Ten kilometres outside the city limits there is a very extensive area known as

159

the Milk Colony. At one stage there was a project to provide milk for the population of Madras from herds of dairy cattle imported from Australia and elsewhere, and pastured just outside Madras. Hundreds and hundreds of acres were set aside for the project, the herds were established and the prospects were good. Then disease struck and the imported cattle were unable to survive. The huge tracts of land set aside for the Milk Colony still exist, and are in marked contrast to the congested slum areas around Vyasarpady. Father Mantovani was able to buy thirty-four acres of land in the district to build a home for his leprosy patients, and in 1966 he transferred the first group of ten to the new site. He deliberately brought out only ten first of all; he was following in his Master's footsteps in setting up this home, and he wanted that to be perfectly clear through the symbolism of bringing ten at the beginning.

Father Mantovani's scheme was implemented in 1966, just three years after the death of John XXIII, so the place was named Pope John's Garden. Father Mantovani did not live long after this himself; his death in 1967 came before many of the existing facilities could be provided, but the inspiration and motivating force were his, as was the basic concept and underlying spirit according to which the complex has been planned. His successor was a Dutchman, Father Schlooez, a dynamic personality who established Pope John's Garden on a sound footing so that it caters for over three hundred patients with leprosy, now known as Hansen's Disease. An important part of the treatment at Pope John's Garden is the policy of building up the self-esteem of the patients. Leprosy spreads more easily in places where there is overcrowding, undernourishment and lack of sanitary facilities; part of the therapy for the patients is to create pleasant, beautiful surroundings and to encourage cleanliness and tidiness. Olive discovered Pope John's

Garden to be one of the most beautiful places she had visited in India. She had seen parts of New Delhi which were quite attractive. As capital of the country and principal venue for foreign diplomats and state visitors, it is maintained in a way that no other Indian city is. To have streets in which flowers are grown in roundabouts, and to have lawn areas on median strips and on verges is virtually unknown elsewhere in the country. But what she had seen in New Delhi was equalled, if not excelled, at Pope John's Garden. Every effort had been made to establish a property and buildings which would be pleasing to the eye. A coconut grove provided the main tree cover, but there were mango trees as well, with flowering bougainvillea adding colour to the scene. The driveway was well maintained, with brick and concrete kerbing along its whole extent. Such things are taken for granted in this country, but it is so rare in India that it was obvious to Olive that a very special effort had been made at Pope John's Garden. It was in marked contrast, for example, to the depressing streets of Vyasarpady and Madavaram through which she had approached the centre. Well tended garden plots bordered each of the buildings, and near the centre of these is a small zoo in which peacocks, rabbits, pigeons and ducks are kept. The provision of an aviary and a miniature zoo is indicative of the spirit in which Pope John's Garden was built. The whole place was designed and built to be aesthetically beautiful as well as functional and serviceable. Most of the people suffering from Hansen's Disease come from depressing, unattractive environments. The realization that they are afflicted with a complaint that may cause terrible disfigurement can be devastating to their morale. Everything is done, therefore, at Pope John's Garden to raise and keep up spirits. From the effort that had been consciously made to provide and maintain beautiful surroundings a visitor gets the impression that the people living in this place must be the most important in India and that nothing is too good for them.

In the chapel more than anywhere else Olive was left with this feeling. In the Christmas season abundant but tasteful decorations hang from the ceiling to supplement the lights festooning the altar and the illuminated crib. Colour and light suffuse the chapel and an atmosphere of peace and joy impresses the visitor as he marvels at the serenity of these people who, with fingers, toes, legs and arms missing, worship their God.

A day spent in the company of the leprosy patients at Pope John's Garden is a humbling and inspiring experience. Not a shred of self-pity, but a spirit of happiness is the overall impression they give. They are eager to show what is to be seen in the place, and they are eager for visitors to discover for themselves why they are so proud of their home and why they are so happy in it.

Those who are able to work are encouraged to do so. A whole variety of activities is provided – shoemaking, tailoring, matmaking, weaving, candlemaking, plaiting coconut leaves into roofing. A poultry run and a thriving piggery are features of the place, and the garden is kept well supplied with plants from the nursery. A part of the thirty-four acres is given over to a rice paddy, but most rice growing takes place at another property of twenty-two acres in a different section of the Milk Colony. Sufficient rice is grown there, under the supervision of Sister Monica, to feed the three hundred patients for nearly seven months of the year. Supplies have to be bought for the rest of the time. A few sheep are also raised on the farm to provide a little meat occasionally.

Depending on what stage the disease has reached when the patients are admitted, they are put in houses, wards, dormitories or the infirmary. Some are able to move around quite freely, others with difficulty; some are bedridden, and a small number need to be accommodated in acute care wards. Despite the fact that most visitors know that leprosy is not contagious, there is an almost instinctive revulsion when a patient puts out a hand with fingers missing to offer a handshake of welcome. It may be quite irrational, but it is none the less quite common for the thought to occur, "Will I contract leprosy as a result of this?"

Olive was quick to sense that the one thing the leprosy patients crave is affection. More than anything they resent the rejection that they experience from so many people. When they come across individuals who accept them, mix with them, identify with them, they take them to their hearts. Olive had the great grace of having no fear whatever of having physical contact with the patients. When she was first taken to Pope John's Garden and joined in the celebration of the Eucharist, the patients stood back and let her go to Communion while they remained at a respectful distance from her. But this was not the spirit of the Eucharist as she understood it – we go to receive Jesus in the Eucharist as brothers and sisters, and this is how she wanted it to be, so she soon got them to be comfortable with her, going to receive together with them, in their very midst. It is an interesting experience to be assisting at the Eucharist with patients for the first time – the initial feeling can be to want to receive the Sacrament last of all out of a sense of reverence for the Crucified and Risen Jesus who is present in the heart of each of these people whom He has brought close to Himself through their suffering. But this can be quickly superseded by the desire to be united with them, to receive together with them, to be in the very midst of them to show symbolically the desire to identify with them.

Olive was close to tears after she came back to her place on receiving Communion, for she saw the priest begin to move amongst the patients who were unable to approach the altar themselves to receive, or who could do so only with difficulty. Just before he reached those completely immobile she saw men and women dragging themselves to the aisle, one with a leg missing, another hobbling over on the stumps of legs amputated at the thighs. She thought of Paul's words about the members of the Body of Christ making up what is lacking in the sufferings of Christ, and her appreciation of the Eucharist as a memorial of the suffering, death and resurrection of Jesus was deepened immeasurably.

In a short time Olive got to know different ones amongst the patients and would hug them and embrace them on arriving and leaving. This more than anything, endeared her to them and she quickly became "Mummy", and in their eyes "Mummy" she will always be. It is intriguing to see men and women today in their fifties and sixties referring to her affectionately in this way.

Sister Sabina and Sister Fatima are still in the community of seven sisters who help run Pope John's Garden, and they remember Olive's visits from "Beatitudes". Originally she would come out for several days, but later she came on day visits each Thursday, when the Rector would take his turn to celebrate Mass there. Paradoxically, a visit to the patients was a welcome break for Olive; not only did she come to a place which was in a beautiful setting with plenty of lush green foliage all around, she was amongst people who really were her friends and who appreciated her deeply. Mary Obargarn testified to the depth of her feeling for Olive when she learnt in 1987 that Olive was suffering from a brain tumour, "If only God would allow me to suffer so that Mummy could be spared."

There were always plenty of things for Olive to interest herself in and enquire about. Several of the patients were skilled at weaving, and made lunghis, bandages, gauze, shirting cloth and towels. Another patient was a shoemaker and made up sandals on the premises. For the patients he used a special material, micro-cellular rubber, a spongy substance which protects anaesthetic feet.

Raman the clerk, who has been at Pope John's Garden for fourteen years, is always keen to teach foreigners a few words of Tamil: "Nandri" – thank you, "Kalai Vanakkam" – good morning, "Thankai" – coconut, "Thanner" – water, etc., etc. Olive found that she could get by with English when in the city, but once in the villages there would be a lot of people who could speak only their own languages. Nearly every state has its own language, so in the three places where Olive had so far spent most of her time, the people had been using Bengali, Hindi and Tamil. The four years she was to spend in Madras meant that Tamil was the most useful language for her, and even the few basic words that Raman could teach were a blessing on occasions. On a hot day, for example, when a drink was needed but a safe water supply was not guaranteed, Olive would buy a green coconut for a rupee. She needed the word "Thankai" if she wanted to find out where coconuts were being sold, but if a pile of coconuts were heaped up on a stall it was enough to point and gesture. The vendor would then slice the top off, supply a straw, and a safe drink was immediately to hand. When she had finished drinking the coconut water she would hand back the coconut, which the vendor would split open so that she could scoop out the soft flesh which had a delightfully smooth, sweet taste.

In the hot season Olive had to be careful to keep up the supply of liquids, because dehydration can easily set in. Geoff Crowther's advice on this score is interesting: "In the hot season you have to balance the dangers of drinking water against the dangers of dehydration. The first is possible, the second is definite, so if necessary, throw caution to the winds and drink more water."

For married couples who are patients, there are small houses in one section of Pope John's Garden. Mothers with young children can be seen there, and in Olive's day children were left with the parents until they were six. They would then be moved into "Beatitudes" and looked after there, with the parents keeping in touch by monthly visits. At present the children are left with the parents and regularly given prophylactic treatment.

The nature of leprosy and its treatment as outlined below was explained by Dr V.D.G. Chandran, an eye, nose and throat specialist who is a consultant physician at Pope John's Garden. He assisted the patients at Mother Teresa's home in Madras until she won the Nobel Prize; then when help began flooding in and numerous volunteers appeared, he switched his allegiance to Pope John's Garden which was not so well known and where help was needed.

Leprosy is caused by bacteria which are very similar to TB bacteria. It affects people who have an immune deficiency, and when suffering from malnutrition they are more susceptible to it. It is not transmitted by heredity. Rather, it is quite common for it to be spread from one person to another through the nasal discharge.

The incubation period of the bacteria can be anything from six months to five years. Previously the treatment given was essentially designed to control the spread of the disease by the use of anti-leprosy drugs. These killed most but not all of the bacteria, but did not eradicate the disease itself. In the last ten to fifteen years bactericidal drugs have been discovered which can eradicate, and not merely control, the bacteria, and new hope has been given to the patients.

From biblical times down to our own day it has been common practice to isolate patients suffering from the disease, and the picture of the warning bells they had to ring is one of the most vivid images that leprosy conjures up. In India rigid isolation of patients has not been widely practised – they remain in the community and are treated as human beings without being totally rejected by being placed on inaccessible islands like Molokai. While this approach has been more humane than an isolationist policy, it has led to the disease spreading more rapidly and more widely. As a result, it is common to find leprosy control centres in country towns as well as in the cities, especially in the states of Andra Pradesh and Tamil Nadu, both in the south of the country. Notices can be seen in buses urging leper patients to report to control centres, and highlighting the fact that leprosy can be cured. One of the most popular films of the last twenty years told the story of a beautiful woman cured by a doctor but still rejected by her family so that she went back to live out her life in the colony. The film had a re-run on national television in November 1986 and was followed by notices on the screen alerting people what to do if leprosy is contracted. It is clear that leprosy is still quite prevalent in parts of the country and still greatly feared.

While doctors can control and even eradicate the disease, they cannot eliminate the deformities which patients have already sustained. Medically speaking, these people are no longer patients but in the eyes of ordinary people the disfigurement they carry is their life sentence. They remain social outcasts; their greatest trial is rejection by people. The inability of their children to marry into families in which there is no leprosy is symptomatic, even though they may mingle ordinarily with the general population in other ways. Hopefully, their children will be totally integrated into normal society.

In the popular mind there is a great deal of misunderstanding based on ignorance; for example, some people working with the children of patients take it for granted, even today, that ninety per cent of them will end up with the disease. In fact only the small number born with the immune deficiency will be affected.

Whatever expert medical opinion about leprosy is, the attitude of the general community is much the same as it ever was. Young men and women born of parents who had leprosy but who themselves do not have the disease find it very difficult to find marriage partners in the general community. Their children may be able to integrate into society, but at least two generations seem to be needed. Occasionally a young man is able to find someone who will marry him but it is extremely rare for a girl to do so.

It is important for the youngsters and their families to build up their level of expectation. Both boys and girls are given a good education at "Beatitudes", and the opportunity for advancement is there, but in general the students do not reach a high degree of learning. As yet, there is no one who has graduated from a university. Given the background from which they come, this is understandable; the boys, for example, tend to get jobs as mechanics, drivers, cycle repairers or the like. There is considerable pressure on the girls to marry at an early age and they follow the pattern, in general, of the community at large.

After Olive had been at "Beatitudes" for some time, something happened which disturbed her greatly. As year followed year, the facilities for the children of the patients proved inadequate and unsatisfactory. Provision was made for the girls, but the housing available for the boys left Olive very dissatisfied. The time came when the only place of shelter for them was with the handicapped. "Surely something better can be done for these youngsters. They deserve better than this!" — the thought was seldom out of her mind but there was just no money. The expenditure on medicines alone was 200,000 rupees a year. At least the boys were alive, were being well fed and well looked after. They did have a roof over their heads, even though they were terribly crowded and living on top of one another. She would just have to do something about it.

26

Visit to Shantivanam
and Quilon

Before Olive came up with a solution to the problem of the
boys' accommodation, she decided to familiarize herself
with some more of South India. Three hundred and thirty
kilometres south of Madras is Tiruchirappalli. In the time of
the Raj the British found they could not get their tongues
around this name and abbreviated it to Trichy, by which it is
commonly known today. Thirty kilometres from Trichy is
the ashram of Shantivanam, directed by Father Bede
Griffiths, an English Benedictine who has been in India for
thirty years, twenty of them at Shantivanam. Olive had
heard of the interesting things being done at the ashram by
way of inculturation – Indian customs were incorporated
into the liturgy as far as possible, and though the ashram
was Christian and its worship quite recognizably Catholic,
people of all religions were welcome. This was just the kind
of thing that intrigued Olive, so when she decided to head
south she thought she would take in the ashram.

The Pallavan Express is an excellent train and the trip
from Madras to Trichy takes four and a half hours. A local
bus for thirty kilometres to Kulittalai along the valley of the
River Carvery is the normal way of reaching Shantivanam,
and an attractive trip it is. Just as the Ganges is the sacred
river for the north of India, the Carvery is the sacred river
for the south. It does not compare favourably with the
Ganges in many respects – though it is a thousand metres

171

wide, the depth of the water is little more than three feet. None the less the river has attracted to its banks a number of temples large and small, and the fertile valley owes its prosperity to irrigation. Plantations of sugar cane alternate with bananas and coconuts, while rice paddies are dotted everywhere. It is a delightful trip, with greenery all the way, and glimpses of the river and irrigation channels to add variety.

Shantivanam means "Forest of Peace" and is appropriately named because it is located on the banks of the Carvery, with a banana plantation next door, coconut palms all around and a eucalyptus grove running along the riverside. Olive did what all visitors are asked to do – attend the ceremonies in chapel three times a day, 6.30 a.m. for Morning Office and Mass, 12.15 for Midday Prayer, and 7.00 p.m. for Evening Prayer. Father Bede is eighty years of age, a world renowned scholar, has lectured widely in many countries and is revered by many as a deeply spiritual man. He attracts people from all over the world, and at any one time there will usually be about thirty people at the ashram. At times like Christmas and Easter there will be as many as a hundred.

Most people find the highlight of the day the five or ten minutes each morning and evening when Father Bede comments on the readings of Scripture which are included in the Eucharist. It is not his learning which comes through, so much as the wisdom of the years and an openness to the Holy Spirit at work in him.

Quite a number of symbols drawn from Hindu tradition are used in the liturgy at Shantivanam. The reason for this is the growing concern of a number of Christians that Christianity has been presented in India in a way that is so overlaid with Western and European customs as to be offputting to Indians. To become Christian, do they have to cease to live as Indians following Indian customs and traditions? When people reflect that Christianity has been in India for two thousand years yet only two per cent of the Indian people are Christian, serious questions suggest themselves. Hence the effort of Father Bede Griffiths and others to strip away the non-essential practices and customs from Christianity and to replace these with corresponding Indian ones.

Olive walked into this situation without any preparation and was shocked at what she found. Arati was one thing. This consists of waving lights or incense about a person or thing as a sign of honour or worship. At the Preparation of the Gifts in the Mass and at the Consecration arati is offered, using incense and grains of camphor which burn away leaving no residue. At the Offertory a fourfold offering is made to God of water, earth, air and fire, exactly as happens in Hindu puja or worship, as a sign of the offering of the elements to God. Water is sprinkled on the altar and on the people to purify them, after which the celebrant takes a sip to purify himself. The fruits of the earth, bread and wine, are offered together with eight flowers which have been placed around them – these represent the eight directions of space, and signify that the Mass is offered in the centre of the universe and thus relates it to the whole of creation; it is a cosmic act in which the whole creation, together with all humanity, is offered through Christ to the Father.

At the end of the Morning Office, when psalms are recited and prayers read, sandal paste is passed around from one to the other so that each one can put a dob of this on his forehead. Sandalwood is considered the most precious of all woods and symbolizes the divinity – it is placed on the head or the hands as a way of signifying the consecration of the body to God.

At the end of Midday Prayers a spot of the powder known as kumkumum is placed between the eyebrows symbolizing "the third eye" or the eye of wisdom. The third eye is the inner eye which sees the inner light – "if thine eye be single thy whole body shall be full of light". This is the same as the third eye which was often added in Greek ikons of Christ and is a universal symbol.

Ashes are placed on the forehead at Evening Prayer because impurities have been burnt away from ash and this signifies that sins and impurities are removed, the ash itself symbolizing the purified self.

This was all rather too much for Olive. It was one thing for Catholic Benedictine monks to dress in the saffron robes of Hindu sannyasis, to sit cross-legged on the floor and to celebrate the Eucharist in this posture, but to introduce the symbolism of arati, sandalwood paste, the third eye, and vibhuti ashes into the liturgy itself was to her tantamount to debasing Christian worship with pagan practices. It seemed to Olive that instead of Christianity being brought to India, Hinduism was assimilating Christianity. She was quite uncomfortable about the whole thing and stayed little more than a day. What is more, she penned to Father Bede a scathing denunciation of what he was doing.

In all of this Olive was experiencing what so many of us experience. We have expressed our faith in God, in the person of Jesus, in the Church, in Christianity, in the same familiar ways for so long that it does not seem possible to do otherwise. The customs and traditional practices which are ways of expressing our faith become identified with faith itself. It can be a painful process to realize that practices and customs which we hold very dear, and which have always been an integral part of our religious experience, are simply that – practices and customs which are not essential to being Christian. The effort some people in India and elsewhere are making to strip away what are merely Western and European customs and practices from the essence of Christianity has caused a lot of heartache and has been accompanied by a lot of criticism and suffering. Olive might have been helped during her visit to Shantivanam had she known that everything that is done there has the approval of the Catholic Bishops' Conference in India.

Five years later Father Bede went on a lecture tour of Australia, during the course of which he gave a television interview. At the same time a Mass which he celebrated incorporating the symbols explained above was videotaped. Olive was in Australia herself by this time and saw all of this on television. By then she had come to understand what he and others were attempting to do, and she was gracious enough to acknowledge that she had not understood what it was all about. She was much more sympathetic and felt she ought to write him another letter to set things right.

Since Olive found little to detain her at Shantivanam, she metaphorically shook its dust off her feet and headed further south. Kanyakumari, also known as Cape Cormorin, is the southernmost tip of India. Here the Bay of Bengal meets the Indian Ocean, and at full moon the Cape affords a visitor the unique experience of seeing the sun set simultaneously with the moon rising over the ocean. Olive headed for Kanyakumari — if that was the most southerly point of India, obviously she had to see it. Once there she found little of interest. The beach was uninspiring, though there was a ferry to Vivekananda Rock, a memorial to one of India's most important religious crusaders, two hundred metres offshore. So she headed next for Quilon in Kerala.

Kerala is quite different from anything Olive had seen in India so far. Calcutta, Delhi and Madras are big, bustling cities with crowds of people at every hand's turn. Cochin with a population of 480,000 is the largest city in Kerala, so it is no wonder that there is a comparatively easy-going, relaxed atmosphere in the state. This was formed in 1956 by combining Travancore, Cochin and Malabar. In the nineteenth century the state of Travancore carried out a far-sighted policy of land distribution, and as a result, land is shared more equitably than in the rest of India. Holdings may not be large, but most people seem to have a plot of ground. Each house is set in a quarter acre of ground or more, with its own coconut palms. From the air cities like Trivandrum or Quilon look like huge coconut plantations — the houses are hidden by the trees which extend mile after mile. This led a recent President of India to describe Kerala on his first visit there as "one huge village". Cultivation is intense and there is none of the grinding poverty that is evident in other parts of India.

Olive stayed for several days in a convent in Quilon, and enjoyed this small market town, with its cashew tree plantations and coconut palms on Ashtamudi Lake. About fifty miles further up the coast Cochin has the reputation of being the Venice of India, but Olive could see canals aplenty around Quilon. The famous backwaters boat trip from Quilon to Alleppey begins in Ashtamudi Lake and wends through delightful canals for a whole day, passing narrow spits of land only yards wide, with home, garden and farmyard animals squeezed in, then through shallow lakes alive with fishermen and on to delightful little settlements on palm fringed lakes or canals. Olive also saw numerous Chinese fishing nets in and around Quilon. These are fixed in one position on the bank and are lowered and raised in and out of the water on a cantilever; she saw then going in and out often enough but did not see many fish caught by this method. However, there was an abundance of fish on the menu and this brought a welcome variety to her diet.

After two weeks away from "Beatitudes" it was time to head back to Madras. A good train service from Quilon to Madurai, then on to Trichy and Madras, solved the perennial problem of "getting there". Olive soon discovered that you do not measure a journey in India by miles or kilometres, but by the number of hours the journey takes. Generally speaking, she preferred train to bus, but there were occasions when there was no choice. She quickly learnt that the most important part of a vehicle for a driver in India is the horn. Country roads have no footpaths and they are used for all kinds of purposes as well as carrying motorized traffic. Bicycles, bullock carts and pedestrians she could have expected, but she did not bargain on the incessant horn-blowing that marked the approach of any one of these. Without exaggeration, during one third of a journey the horn would be going, and with the strident noise blaring for half-minute to minute intervals at a time, there was a lot to be said for travelling by train. She was intrigued by other uses to which roads were put, too. Some enterprising farmers would strew their rice stalks across the road up to two or three inches deep. Cars, trucks and buses running over it winnowed the grain and saved the trouble of putting it through machines or threshing it by hand. A strip of road a metre or so wide would sometimes be marked off with stones or bricks, warning vehicles to avoid that patch; this was not to alert drivers to a hazardous section of roadway, but rather to signify that nuts or grain or some other commodity was being dried out, so please avoid! Another experience Olive had not come across in other countries was the occasional use of elephants to collect money from bus passengers. Elephants are quite commonly kept in temples and they also show up in country towns from time to time. It is a little unnerving to be sitting in a bus minding one's own business only to find a trunk snaking its way through the window and waiting for a coin to be tendered. People invariably do offer something, which is skilfully taken in the tip of the trunk and passed to the mahout; there is always the fear that the elephant will wrap its trunk around a person so ungracious as to not offer anything and whisk the offender out of the bus.

A feature of travelling that Olive had to learn to cope with in India was the beggars. When buses and trains pull up at stops for a few minutes it is common for beggars to get on and work their way through the vehicle. Taxis approaching set-down points like an Air India booking office are prime targets – beggars wait at traffic lights and other vantage points and thrust maimed or deformed limbs into the car. Mothers carrying emaciated babies pluck at travellers' sleeves or arms and try to shame people into giving. Children are organized into groups and ply assigned areas, dogging visitors' footsteps, almost hounding them at times. A white face attracts immediate attention and normally signifies a person who has unlimited resources compared to the beggar. Beggars' unions are formed with well defined beats, the organizers creaming off a goodly percentage of the takings. Even some people who can support themselves will ask for money if they come across "an easy touch". The usual advice to Westeners is not to give money to beggars in public – this merely encourages the practice and perpetuates the problem. Edna Vawser is a missioner of the Church of Christ who left Australia in the 1920s and has devoted over sixty years of her life to alleviating suffering and poverty in Barramati near Pune. She has done extraordinary work and given her whole life in selfless devotion to the people of the area. She cites the case of a beggar at the railway station in Barramati who collapsed at his post. He was taken to hospital where the preliminary examination showed he needed surgery urgently. He pleaded to be given the money to pay for his hospital expenses before the anaesthetic was administered – yet the nurses found strapped to his body under his rags more money than was needed to pay for all his expenses! Edna does not give money to beggars but she devotes her whole life and what resources she has to assisting the poor and needy. Mother Teresa does not dispense money on the streets to professional beggars – she brings effective aid to people who are in genuine need. However, foreigners are at a disadvantage in dealing with this problem, and find it difficult to distinguish genuine cases from phoneys.

Sometimes it is all too obvious, though, as in the case of a Calcutta woman at Babu Ghat. This is several miles from Shishu Bhavan and the area where Olive stayed when with the Missionaries of Charity.

There is a tea stand at the stop for bus 76 at Babu Ghat overlooking the Hoogly River, and this woman was scrabbling through the pile of refuse accumulated from the scraps thrown there. When a man from the tea stand emptied a teapot onto the ground she scooped up some of the tea with one of the discarded clay cups and drank it on the spot. This was too much for a bystander, who thrust a five rupee note into her hand so that she could buy some rice and get a wholesome meal inside her. The woman accepted the money but she was not to be deterred from her immediate goal – she went on fossicking through the putrefying food for a few mouthfuls.

What did Olive make of all this? No matter what explanations were given, no matter what number of con men were operating, it was still clear that there was a huge number of people who were in desperate need. Certainly prudence was needed to see that money and resources were effectively used, but that was no justification for doing nothing. What a fearful thing if this could be said of her:

TOUCHED BY GOD

I was hungry but you would not feed me,
thirsty but you would not give me a drink;
I was a stranger but you would not welcome me
in your home,
naked but you would not clothe me;
I was sick and in prison,
but you would not take care of me. *(Matthew 25:42-43)*

27

Questing in Australia

The plight of the boys at "Beatitudes" who had been left without satisfactory accommodation plagued Olive, and she continued to mull over what might be done. At this time she was spending increasingly long periods in prayer and was often to be found sitting in her wheelchair in the chapel. She continued her usual activities, though, her weekly visit to Pope John's Garden, her visits to the old people and to the not so old. She discovered one lady who was alert enough to be able to follow chess, and so introduced her to the intricacies of the game.

The wheelchair that she used initially was of the ordinary type, and she either propelled herself around if she was indoors, or she would have some of the boys push her over to the old people's ward. The big yard in "Beatitudes" was covered with sand in parts and did not make for easy progress in a wheelchair. She sometimes came out of the chair, too, when it got onto uneven ground or when she was accidentally tipped out. This happened once when she was near the old people's wards; she struck her face and bled profusely. Those who were aware of what had happened were very concerned, but Olive in her usual way made nothing of it.

When Olive had settled into "Beatitudes" and had become part of the place, a four-wheeler chair was constructed for her. This gave her greater mobility and she as able to propel herself about. By means of this she was able to venture outside "Beatitudes" and get along to the market, which she enjoyed. She also managed to tip herself into a ditch, but as usual this was just par for the course, nothing to write home about and certainly nothing to make a fuss of.

Sister Agatha was the principal of the school attached to "Beatitudes" and she would invite Olive to present prizes to the students when occasions presented themselves. The Sisters had her over to the Convent to celebrate her seventy-ninth birthday, and quite a fuss was made of her by all and sundry at times like this.

All the while she was thinking of "her boys", and gradually she came to the conclusion that she was the one who ought to raise the money needed to build them a home. She did not come to that decision quickly or lightly; she prayed a good deal over the matter and talked it over with Father Ittyachen, but once the decision was taken there was no holding her. She would go to Australia and raise the money. Where would she go? How would she go about it? These details were not clear, in fact Olive had little or no idea of these things. She simply had the conviction that she ought to do it, that this was what God wanted of her.

So the next thing we find is that Olive is Australia bound. Her goal: $40,000. Getting on and off buses and trains is hard enough for an invalid; negotiating aeroplanes is another matter. Olive had quickly adapted to being swung aloft in a wheelchair on the mobile hoist and, if anything, found planes easier to cope with than buses and trains. A stopover at Singapore enabled her to have a good rest in one of the rooms that for $10 a day Singapore Airlines provide transit passengers with. Then it was on to Perth and her questing tour had begun.

When she had driven through Madras on the way to the airport, buses, rickshaws, pedestrians and the occasional cow had been vying for space. Vendors were displaying their wares on footpaths and even spilling on to the streets, while beggars patiently plied their trade. The contrast in Perth, as Olive was whisked from the plane through free-ways and alongside the Canning River, was overwhelming. Yachts and launches were rocking gently at anchor as she drove by, and the realization that millions of dollars had been invested in those pleasure craft hit her fair and square between the eyes. She could not rid herself of the sight of the eight hundred people coming to "Beatitudes" daily for their bowl of rice – the cost of any one of these boats she was passing would have sustained the family of one of these people for a lifetime.

Olive did not allow herself to be thrown off balance by such thoughts but gave herself to the task in hand. Dafne and Peter Jones welcomed her to Perth and gave her the hospitality of their home. Various members of the family had visited "Beatitudes" and were familiar with the work being done there. Dafne was amongst Olive's strongest supporters – she had put her in touch with people, organ-ized fund-raising activities and arranged for Olive to be interviewed on TV. The family came to know Olive very well and realized that she had a healthy appetite and a penchant for good food – they realized too just what Olive had given up in this regard, with rice as her staple diet in India.

After Perth came Adelaide and Olive almost burst on to the Adelaide scene. Providentially she had made contact with Helen Astbury, a liaison officer in the Catholic Media, who put her in touch with the Religious Affairs writer of the morning daily paper. Peter White realized he was on to a good story, and on Saturday, 18th September, a front page article together with a photograph of Olive appeared in *The Advertiser*. It read as follows:

AT 77, OLIVE SET OFF TO HELP INDIA'S POOR

"ALL IT TAKES IS LOVE"

At 77 and comfortably settled in a Toowoomba retirement home, Mrs Olive Allerton decided to leave family and friends and join a church mission team in the slums of India.

The fact that she had been on crutches for a year after the onset of a muscular disease did not deter Mrs Allerton.

Widowed seven years earlier, she put her affairs in order and, without telling her two children, who lived in other states, until the day before her departure, she flew out of Australia to join Mother Teresa's team in Calcutta.

Now 79, she is back in Australia briefly to raise $40,000 for a boys' home for the Roman Catholic Beatitudes Social Welfare Centre, Madras, where she has lived and worked for the past year.

The article concluded by indicating that Olive would be speaking at a church hall the following evening. There Olive spoke about the work of "Beatitudes" and Pope John's Garden. She did not speak for long, approximately twenty minutes, but she made quite an impact. That was the beginning of a series of speaking engagements that went on for the best part of three months off and on, during the next year. The immediate result was for her to be invited to speak to the students of Rostrevor College, a Christian Brothers' School in Adelaide. The Christian Brothers then took up her cause and gave her contacts in Victoria and New South Wales and later on in Western Australia.

In Adelaide, Olive was staying with her daughter Jean and her husband Michael, and an amusing incident occurred when Olive took a bath at their home. At this stage, Olive was a big woman, and the bath was a small one, so small that Olive became jammed in it. The most strenuous efforts of Jean and Olive herself to get out were unavailing; neighbours had to be summoned and four people were needed to extricate Olive unceremoniously from the bath. Ever afterwards Olive was careful about taking baths — it was much easier to sit on a plastic or metal chair under a shower and freshen up that way!

Before Olive left Adelaide the Christian Brothers in Melbourne undertook to arrange accommodation for her. Father Hinton, whom she thought was in Melbourne, had been transferred to Sydney. In the meantime letters had gone to Archbishop Little and Cardinal Freeman in Melbourne and Sydney respectively. The Brothers would have been able to get her to their schools without any difficulty, but there are always so many requests for fundraising activities that it is important to co-ordinate these with diocesan and statewide charities such as Project Compassion, Catholic Charities Appeal and Freedom from Hunger. Olive was received by Archbishop Little and Cardinal Freeman when she arrived in Melbourne and Sydney and they were happy for her to launch her appeal in their dioceses.

Ten thousand dollars had already come in when Olive flew out of Adelaide. She received a further $2,000 from Parade College in Melbourne, and Brother Simon Nash arranged for her to be taken to schools in Ballarat, Colac, Warrnambool and Geelong. He also set up an interview with *The Advocate*, the Melbourne Catholic paper, but moves to have her appear with Bert Newton on the Don Lane Show on TV came to nothing. However, the media did become aware of her presence, and radio interviews were held and magazine articles began appearing wherever Olive spent a few days. This happened spontaneously and was not the result of carefully prepared press releases being fed to the media. It was just a snow-balling effect.

Brother Simon Nash passed Olive on to Brother Laurie Needham at Waverley College in Sydney, and he saw to transport, accommodation and speaking engagements there. Time was beginning to run out now, and Olive naturally wanted to see her son Bill at Rydal, a tiny settlement ten miles out of Lithgow and a hundred miles west of Sydney. She spent several days with Bill and his wife Gill, and then returned to Sydney. The appeal which had begun so well in Adelaide did not have the same success in its latter stages. Australia was in the grip of a very severe drought, the worst in living memory, so that money was becoming tighter all the time. Father Phillip Crotty, an Australian Jesuit, was home from India and he too was appealing for funds at precisely the same time, in his case for the Hazaribagh Mission. The school year was also coming to a close — senior students had already left school, other students were now in the throes of exams, and it was no longer feasible to visit schools. Olive flew back to Adelaide and by mid-December was making ready to return to Madras. She had collected $30,000. It was not the $40,000 she had been aiming for, but it was enough to make a start. Furthermore, she had made some very good friends, amongst whom were Joe and Pat Gareffa. They lived in Norton Summit in the hills just outside Adelaide, and had undertaken to collect any money that was sent in for "Beatitudes" and forward it to Olive. Cheques and money orders were still coming in as a result of the radio interviews and newspaper articles featuring Olive's work. It was while Olive was at the home of Joe and Pat that she was asked whether she would come back to Australia again to continue the appeal. Quick as a flash, she replied, "Oh yes, I would come again."

The thought behind the question was not so much that of raising money; the additional $10,000 could have been raised in Australia if a sufficient number of people had set their minds to it seriously. It would have been hard work and it would have been more difficult without Olive, but it could have been done. What was in mind, was the impact that Olive had been making on people. Wherever she went the result was invariably the same: "If she can do that at the age of seventy-nine as a semi-invalid, what am I doing?"

28

Interlude at MITHRA

On returning to India Olive soon found herself at MITHRA, which she had come to know of before her first trip to Australia from "Beatitudes". MITHRA was the Madras Institute to Habilitate Retarded and Afflicted, and had been founded by Sister Theodore, an Australian nun from Queensland. Sister Theodore can be best described as a modern-day feminine Friar Tuck. She is a merry person with a heart as big as her not inconsiderable frame, and with boundless confidence in God's providential care. When retarded and handicapped children needed a home she took over a swampy block of land in the suburb of Anna Nagar, had it drained and levelled, and erected the first building. The children needing help were very severely handicapped and Sister Theodore enlisted the assistance of a number of young women whom she trained for this work. Seven of these are now doing their novitiate year and hopefully will form the nucleus of a new religious community to continue Sister Theodore's work. Olive learnt of all this when she was searching out some place where specialist help could be given to two of the boys at "Beatitudes".

When the building programme at "Beatitudes" reached the stage where Olive had to leave her room, she moved over to MITHRA temporarily and was given a room in the children's quarters. MITHRA was a much smaller establishment than "Beatitudes" — there were fifty resident children, eighty-five in remedial classes and twenty-five receiving various types of therapy. The children in therapy required individual attention, those in classes were taught in small groups. Olive identified with MITHRA while she was there, just as she had with "Beatitudes", but her first stay was not a prolonged one. Back at "Beatitudes" in a new room, it was not long before Olive fell sick. Father Ittyachen had in the meantime been transferred to Sacred Heart College in Tiruppatur, over a hundred miles from Madras. Olive was sorry to lose a friend and confidant in him, but in time came to have a working relationship with the new Director, Father Tarcisius. This did not happen immediately, for he could see very little of her, as she was forced to spend long periods in bed, was perpetually tired, and seemed to be experiencing a reaction to the rigorous itinerary she had given herself when in Australia. In fact she may have been experiencing the first effects of the brain tumour which was not diagnosed until some months later.

Olive's condition worsened and she was admitted to hospital. She was not impressed with the treatment she received, gave several of the doctors very short shrift and discharged herself. In spite of herself she was taken back to hospital, but once again, as soon as she could manage she left, long before the doctors considered her to be in a fit condition to go home. In this situation it was felt the best place for Olive was MITHRA. Father Tarcisius and the staff from "Beatitudes" had been visiting her daily in hospital, but would not have been able to give Olive the attention she needed if she had been at "Beatitudes". Two women at MITHRA were able to do this, Saroja and Siria Pushpam, and they had to give Olive almost constant attention. It was months before Olive became right again, during which time Father Tarcisius was becoming established at "Beatitudes".

INTERLUDE AT MITHRA

While Olive was at MITHRA there arrived from Australia, on 25th March 1983, a Dominican nun, Sister Patricia. Her coming to India was a direct result of Olive's first talk in Adelaide at St Cecilia's Hall. Sister Patricia had retired from teaching and was at the end of her active life. That Sunday night, having been inspired by what Olive had done, as she lay in bed before going to sleep she thought, "If she can do it, why can't I?" She visited Olive at Jean's home, found out something about both "Beatitudes" and MITHRA, and wrote off to Sister Theodore. The letter that came back said she would be very welcome, but rather than coming immediately could she first of all learn something about Bliss Symbolics? On enquiry Sister Patricia discovered that a course at Regency Park in Adelaide gave a course in Bliss Symbolics, which is a means of enabling deaf and hearing-impaired people to communicate. They spell out words to a tutor by pointing to letters arranged in a square tablet. In less than six months after Olive arrived in Adelaide, Sister Patricia was at MITHRA and able to tutor the staff there in the use of Bliss Symbolics. She is still with Sister Theodore and, like Olive herself, has discovered a whole new career in her retirement. As a senior citizen in Australia she had been pensioned off as having finished her life's work. Now in India she has opened up to deaf mutes the possibility of breaking out of their prison of silence and communicating with other people.

Although Olive had been asked whether she would be willing to come back to Australia, nothing was done to bring this about until the Apex Club of Norwood began looking for ways of helping unemployed young people. John Ordon, a teacher at Rostrevor College, alerted the staff to the fact that Apex did have several thousand dollars which it was willing to put to this use and was keen to hear of ideas. A number of suggestions were made by the staff concerning unemployed youth, and as a rider the proposal was made that Apex pay for Olive's return air fare from Madras. The club took up the idea and in no time things were taking shape. Hans Oldenhove and Stephen Lavis were the moving spirits, and arrangements were made to bring Olive to Australia in July. Apex Clubs in South Australia were alerted and schools – state, independent and Catholic – were circularized. There was such interest in South Australia that it was decided not to worry about the Eastern States. Provision was made to fly Olive to Sydney so that she could spend some time with Bill and Gill at Rydal, but no speaking engagements were arranged.

Three weeks before Olive was due to leave, she became ill again. She was given a blood transfusion and by rights should have remained in Madras. The indomitable will which she displayed throughout her life came into its own again – she willed herself to get back on her feet and no one in Madras was able to prevent her taking that plane. She had a mission to accomplish – the task had been begun, but it was only half done and she was the only one who could complete it. The very prospect of doing something worth while for God and for her beloved boys buoyed her up and set the adrenalin racing. Olive brought mind to bear over matter and so flew into Adelaide airport on Wednesday, 22nd June.

The welcoming party included the President of Norwood Apex Club, Hans and Stephen. Hans had sent out a press release this time to city and country TV and radio stations and to the metropolitan newspapers. This attracted a TV crew from Channel 10, and a reporter and photographer from *The News*. The night Olive arrived in Adelaide there was a segment on the evening TV bulletin, so all Channel 10 viewers became aware of Olive's reappearance in Australia. A number of Apex families hosted Olive in different ways during the next month – she stayed several days with the Lavis and Tyson families; she was entertained to dinner by the D'Souzas, and she was ferried to speaking engagements by Hans. It was intended that the first two or three days in Australia be left free so that Olive could rest after her flight and gather strength for the coming month. However, radio stations were anxious to capitalize on the interest generated by the TV news clip on Channel 10 and an article in *The News*, so Olive was in fact occupied for a good part of those first few days.

Then began quite an odyssey. Several of the Apex Clubs had arranged for her to speak at their meetings. The first of these was at a dinner in the Adelaide Hills, while the following day there was a Saturday afternoon meeting at Golden Grove. When Olive's turn to speak came she was pushed forward in her wheelchair, then four men lifted her bodily on to the stage, chair and all, and she was settled in front of a microphone. Without a note she began telling them of India, of the job and happiness of people who had scarcely a rupee to bless themselves with, of the unfailing hospitality she experienced on all sides, of the Home for the Dying in Calcutta run by Mother Teresa, of the faith and resilience of the leprosy patients, and of the plight of their children. Olive never used a note when she was speaking and she never prepared a set speech. She did prepare herself, however, by entrusting herself and what she had to say to the Holy Spirit. She carried out to the letter Jesus' instruction to the apostles: " . . . do not worry what you are going to say or how you will say it; when the time comes, you will be given what you will say. For the words you will speak will not be yours; they will come from the Spirit of your Father speaking through you" (Matthew 10:19-20).

Olive was conscious of the fact that what she had to say impressed people, set them thinking, made an impact on them. She was equally conscious that this was not simply her doing, it was the power of God working through her. This enabled her to speak of God quite naturally and unaffectedly to mixed audiences of believers and non-believers alike. She did not talk to them about the existence of God; she had no need to — she was living witness, in her own person and in what she had done, to the enabling power of God.

Golden Grove was followed by a daily round of talks and trips. The co-ordinating committee had planned to have Olive involved in no more than one engagement per day, given her age and disabilities. A rest day each week was also included. They did not count on Olive, though. When people rang and asked whether she would come here and speak there, the answer was always "YES". Ten days in the city were followed by a trip to the Riverland — Waikerie, Glossop, Loxton and Renmark, all on the River Murray, were taken in during one week, with the Catholic Women's League, High Schools, Service Clubs and the Riverland TV station all figuring in the programme. Back to Adelaide for another round of city engagements and then off to the Iron Triangle — Whyalla, Port Augusta and Port Pirie. Back again to Adelaide and more city commitments, with forays to nearby country centres on day trips.

When in the Riverland, Olive stayed several nights at Berri in the Home for Old People run by the Sisters of Charity. They were very concerned at her condition and could see the toll that the demanding schedule was taking of her. They did what they could to get her to rest, but once Olive had the bit between her teeth there was no stopping her.

Mindful of the problem that Olive had in extricating herself from the bath while Jean was on her first tour, the organizers of the visit had the foresight to arrange for a trained nurse to assist in bathing or showering Olive each day. This arrangement did not last long, however. When the trained sister provided by the District Nursing Association turned up on the very first day, Olive quickly sent her packing. If she could travel halfway round the world she should be able to organize getting herself cleaned up! "Did you think I smelt", she asked. Olive was nothing if not forthright, and she did not baulk at a frank comment or question when she thought it was called for.

Olive had come to Australia because she was concerned at the plight of her boys not having satisfactory accommodation. She wanted to raise funds to build them a home, but she never mentioned money and she never made a direct appeal. None the less the money flowed in — organizations that she addressed, school groups, individuals, reached into their coffers and sent along money both while she was in Australia and after she returned to India. In all, $70,000 was raised, so that eventually a much bigger building than originally planned rose in the grounds of "Beatitudes".

As July drew to a close, so Olive's stay in Adelaide came to an end. On the last Sunday morning a farewell barbeque was held for the members of the Norwood Apex Club to enable her to say goodbye. The next day she flew off to Sydney for a quick visit to Rydal and then it was on to Perth. Here another Christian Brother, Peter St John, had undertaken to co-ordinate her visit. Accommodated by the St John of God Sisters in the convent attached to their hospital in Perth, Olive was in good hands while in Western Australia and there was no need to worry about getting nurses in to help bathe her! Her visit to Perth was as successful as that to Adelaide, and when she was ready to fly back to

Madras she was well satisfied with the generous response of the Perth people. This compensated in some way for the impression she had received on arriving in Perth the first time. Having come direct from the slums of Madras, she could not but wonder at the huge sums of money spent on yachts and other craft at their moorings in the Canning River, and the furrowed, worried looks of so many people going about the Perth business district. Was that the price of all this affluence? Who was happier – the upwardly mobile middle class of Australia, or her waifs and strays at "Beatitudes"?

29

The last question

Olive returned to what was now her home, "Beatitudes", and tried to resume her normal routine: daily Mass at 6.30 a.m., weekly visits to Pope John's Garden, visits twice a day to the old people's wards, private personal prayer in the chapel or elsewhere, a quiet chat with the boys in the evening after they had finished their study, with an occasional talk to the assembled group as part of night prayers. A tradition established by St John Bosco and faithfully maintained by the Salesians in "Beatitudes" was a homely talk at night, just before bedtime and immediately after the Rosary. The boys recite the Rosary walking around the courtyard and down towards the front gate, accompanied by the priests and brothers. Olive was unable to accompany them as they did this, but would wait at the shrine of Our Lady outside the main office where Night Prayer is concluded. Staff members take it in turn to give the nightly talk, and for a while Olive was able to participate in this too.

But soon after her return she had to abandon this routine. In Australia she had embarked on a punishing programme. Sheer willpower drove her on while she was in the country and while there was an urgent job to be done. At times she was dropping with exhaustion, as, for example, on the day she returned from a visit to a country school at Riverton, to be whisked off to a prayer meeting that night in Tranmere. The effort she made on that particular evening was later rewarded when a large number of cartons of clothing arrived at "Beatitudes", given by the people of Tranmere and packed up and freighted to Madras by Helen and Alan Tyson, with whom she had been staying. Dogged determination carried her through when most others would have called it a day. Father Ittyachen described her as a woman with enormous drive and a challenging nature, who herself responded to a challenge. Difficulties she brushed aside; personal pain and hardship were of little consequence. One night at MITHRA she was on her crutches, making her way slowly from the residence, when she fell over. Sister Patricia was nearby and describes her as having "slowly subsided to the ground. She laughed at herself for not being able to get up and said 'Hello, Mr Moon' as she lay there waiting for help to arrive." She was something like a Galapagos turtle on its back — helplessly incapable of righting herself on her own. Sister Patricia summoned Brothers Donald and Julius, two Franciscans who were helping out at MITHRA at the time, and the three of them got Olive right way up again.

The Sisters of Charity at Berri had rightly been concerned at the toll the trip had been taking of Olive. The drive and determination with which she had forced herself along in Australia had exhausted all her reserves of energy by the time she got back to Madras. The spirit had had its way while on tour; now the flesh clamoured for its due and Olive had a relapse. For weeks she was in a state of exhaustion, and only slowly did she recuperate.

A big boost to her morale was the erection of the building for which she had worked so hard and so perseveringly. The boys had been living in the same quarters as the handicapped; now they were able to move into their building and have something they could call their own. Olive was content that her major work had been accomplished. She could see bricks and mortar in front of her and a fine building that would do any institution proud; what she could not see, and what was infinitely more important, were the stirrings in the hearts and minds and consciences of thousands of people throughout Australia. If Gandhi had witnessed what Olive and scores of others like her had done in his own country — the Mother Teresas, the Edna Vawsers, the Father Mantovanis — would his answer have been the same to that question which had set Olive on her way: "What do you think of Christianity?"

*

In January 1985 Olive fell sick again and this time it was more serious than ever before. One night she got out of bed to go to the toilet, fell over and could not get up again. She called out to the night watchman, who in turn called two of the Sisters. They got her off the floor but needed more help to get her back into bed. For two weeks she remained in bed, attended by Drs Santa and Kala. There was no improvement over this period, so she went into Guest Hospital in Chetpet. This did not prove satisfactory and she was moved into Apollo Hospital. Olive's condition deteriorated further, despite constant care and vigilance. Two volunteers from "Beatitudes", Phil, an Irish girl about twenty-five years old, and Dr Mark, an American doctor, were in constant attendance, while the faithful Lily was always there. Olive went into a coma and the diagnosis was serious; she had a tumour of the brain. Surgery was suggested, but the question was, should it be done on the spot or in Australia? So that her family could be nearby in the emergency it was decided to fly Olive to Australia for treatment. Dr Mark accompanied her in the plane, and within days of the decision being taken Olive found herself in the Royal Adelaide Hospital. Dr Mark remained in Adelaide as long as it was necessary to settle Olive in and then returned to Madras.

Olive came out of the coma temporarily soon after she arrived in Adelaide. Jean had been advised of the situation, of course, and was in to see her each day. In the early visits after Olive regained consciousness she was bright, carrying on a breezy conversation in a very animated style which completely belied the seriousness of her condition. The Adelaide doctors decided against operating; although the tumour was benign it was very serious, and it was thought best to leave it untouched. There were other complications too – high blood pressure, heart trouble, and the spreading muscular dystrophy.

Bill travelled from New South Wales, but by the time he arrived Olive had lost all sense of where she was and a distressing time began for everyone. Bill remained a week and at no stage was he able to communicate with his mother. She was *non compos mentis*, hovering between life and death, and began having all sorts of illusions. For some reason she got it into her head that she had been brought to a brothel. Visitors coming in were clients, and the Sister in charge of the ward was the "Madame". Olive did not take kindly to the situation and tried to drive off the "Madame" by throwing a plate of porridge at her! The mental anguish Olive must have gone through during that period can only be imagined. Jean and Bill felt it very keenly, particularly as Bill had to go back to Rydal without seeing Olive come out of that state. After three weeks in hospital the doctors indicated that they could do no more for Olive. She was to be discharged and put into a Nursing Home.

Jean and her husband Michael were greatly assisted by the social workers at the hospital in finding a place for Olive, and were able to have her admitted to the Lewis Nursing Home on Portrush Road in Beulah Park. This was conveniently located about three miles from where they lived, so Jean was able to keep up her daily visits. For another three or four weeks Olive was drifting in and out of consciousness and could not carry on an intelligible conversation. Then she gradually improved and in time returned to normal. Within another month or two she was back to something like her usual self, taking an interest in life, wheeling herself around the home, and getting to know the other patients.

The one thing she missed most of all was a chapel where she could go to pray and participate in daily Mass. For the previous four years she had been living with a religious community and had been able to assist at the Eucharist and receive Communion daily. A chapel in the nursing home would have been a blessing because Olive had very little privacy, sharing a room with another lady, Mrs Evans. The day room was next to hers and most of the patients spent a good deal of the day there, with the TV on a lot of the time. There was a garden at the back of the home, and a small courtyard, so Olive did have somewhere to retreat to, but she did hanker after the haven that a chapel provides.

About half a mile from the Lewis Nursing Home are two religious houses, the headquarters of the Sisters of St Joseph and a community of Jesuits with their church, St Ignatius. Olive soon discovered this and immediately asked if she could be taken regularly to Mass at St Ignatius. Enquiries were made – first Jean was to be consulted: "Did she think this was wise?"; then there was Matron: "Was Olive in a condition to cope with this?"; next was the doctor: "Would there be any risk involved?" This rigmarole was taking far too long for Olive; she organized herself to be pushed over to Mass one day and afterwards called over a youth aged sixteen: "I say, I want to get to Mass here regularly each Sunday. Do you think you could arrange for some young people to push me over here from the Lewis Nursing Home?" Olive always believed in the direct approach and once again she had fallen on her feet. For the next two years Alex took her to Mass each Sunday and he introduced her to the Norwood Youth Group. There was a Mass at 5.00 each Sunday afternoon and this is the one she attended. The young people came to know Olive sitting in her wheelchair at the front of the Church, Sunday after Sunday. Olive became one of them and joined in their activities as far as she could. They would occasionally have a buffet meal after Mass, followed by a social. On one occasion Olive took great delight in leading off all those teenagers with her wheelchair at the head of the line as they did the snake dance.

In time Olive built up a number of contacts. Helen and Alan Tyson kept in close touch, the Sisters of St Joseph brought her Communion one day each week, Father Farmer from St Ignatius did so another day, and on Tuesday each week she was driven to Goodwood where Mass was celebrated for a charismatic group. Jean was always popping in and taking her for a drive to the beach or getting her home for a meal. Olive by this time had completely lost the use of her legs and was in a wheelchair all the time. But this did not stop her getting about — she would have the wheelchair placed as near as possible to the front seat of a car (a big car, mind you) with the door wide open. By hoisting herself out of the chair and supporting her weight on the door, she would ease herself into the seat. Depending on how she slumped into position and depending, too, on how far she had to go, she would either remain where she was, though this often looked very uncomfortable, or struggle to get into a more upright position. Even at eighty-three the grass was not going to grow under Olive's feet. She used to turn up at all kinds of functions when she could get people to take her, and often enough when people would not take her. One day a friend had arranged to take her to the

Carmelite convent at Glen Osmond, but when the day proved to be unreasonably hot she rang up and cancelled the visit. Olive was disappointed but said nothing; instead she rang for a taxi and took herself there. Similarly, when Bishop Cormac Murphy O'Connor, co-chairman of the ARCIC group (Anglican Roman Catholic International Commission) was visiting Adelaide from England, she organized herself over to the other side of the city by taxi, and had no inhibitions about asking the driver to push her from the car park into the meeting hall.

Olive was not long in the Lewis Nursing Home before she got to know everybody, patients and staff. Throw a group of people together and within a short time the gregarious ones are hail-fellow-well-met with everyone. Olive was certainly gregarious, but the relationships she established were not superficial ones. She could sense the needs of people in the Home, and as always did what she could to help. Birdie was a lady so thin and emaciated that she was as bad as any patient brought in to Mother Teresa's Home for the Dying. She was just wasting away, waiting for death, without the will to live. She would lie in bed hour after hour, staring vacantly into space, unable to speak, suffering the loneliness of the isolation that old age brings to some. Olive would go to Birdie's room, sit by her bedside, clasp her hand and pray quietly for her. Day after day this went on and Olive became quite attached to Birdie. She would sometimes say a few words, but usually there was silent communion between the two. When the end was evidently drawing near Olive wanted to know whether Birdie was conscious of her presence. She leant over her and said, "Birdie, do you know me?" The faintest of whispers came back, "Yes, I do. You love me." Tears were in Olive's eyes as she told this when Birdie had passed on, sped on her way with the Lord's Prayer that Olive said over her.

George was another patient Olive visited, this time at the request of Hank who was responsible for the nursing side of the home. George was suffering from cancer, had gone into hospital for additional surgery, and when he came back most of his nose and part of his mouth had been cut away. He was kept in a room by himself away from the other patients who were normally not permitted to see him. It was almost a matter of course that Olive would be asked to give him some company. And if she had not been asked she would have sought him out.

The nurses, too, realized that they could confide in Olive, and some of them sought her advice on family problems.

Before long Olive was exercising pastoral care for a number of people in the Home. She still hankered to be somewhere else where there was a chapel and daily Mass, but she came to realize that there was a reason for her to remain at Lewis Nursing Home, too.

For quite some time Olive had been associating with people who were close to death. She herself had nearly died when she was flown from Madras to Adelaide, and for some weeks it was touch and go. Now that she had recovered, in some measure at least, how did she feel about death?

In the early stages she was apprehensive and fearful. She felt that there was still so much she should do for God before she appeared before Him. She had done certain things in her life, yes, but there were so many other things she could have done, that she could still do.

Even at eighty-two and eighty-three it seemed that Olive could still grow. She had responded throughout her life to the calls God made. Endowed with an adventurous spirit she had been full of innocent mischief as a child and a young girl, but she had also been conscious of God in her life. When she had fallen in love with Richard Fallowes and expected to be the wife of a clergyman, she went off to

Oxford House to learn about religious matters and experience an ordered life of prayer and good works. Her religious sensitivity was sharpened through her association with Francis Chudoba, and when Neville Allerton swept her off her feet she moved from upper-class circles into the more prosaic, mundane world of mother and housewife. Her youthful dreams of high adventure were replaced by the day to day chores of keeping house. Then came the saga of Kenya and Tanzania, begun with such high hopes only to end in financial difficulty and the death of Neville. A general store and post office in Queensland followed by retirement to Symesthorpe, and then the climax of all that had gone before – India, Mother Teresa's Home for the Dying, and "Beatitudes". Yet there was one more mountain to scale – that of self-acceptance, of taking herself as she was, bringing herself before God with all her inadequacies as well as her achievements, putting herself in His hands and saying: "Here I am, Lord. Take me as I am. I have done for You what I could and now the time has come when I can do no more. Into your hands I commend my spirit."

Olive did not come easily to this. She had to struggle and pray to be able to stand before God empty-handed, as she felt, and yet know that He loved her for all that. A friend gave her a copy of de Caussade's *Self-Abandonment to Divine Providence* and that helped. She had offered herself to God, she had prayed that He might lay the cross on her shoulders, only to discover that the total loss of the use of her legs was a sore trial to endure. Her days and nights were a mixture of pain and joy as her tumour waxed and waned. If she had been in pain and Jean subsequently asked what kind of a night she had had, she would often say, "Like the curate's egg – part good, part bad." She was obviously in considerable pain quite often, but she did not make a song and dance about it.

What she did regret was that Sue Meldrum was no longer able to take her off each Tuesday for the celebration of the Eucharist with the Goodwood Prayer Group. Sue was as willing as ever, but Olive's condition began to deteriorate even further early in 1988. The efforts of Jean and Sue combined may have been sufficient to lift her physically from the wheelchair to car, but they could do nothing to prevent the increasingly frequent periods when the will could no longer drive a rebellious body. Increasing pressure on the brain left Olive in a comatose condition, and on 18th May the body could take no more.

Olive Allerton had fought the good fight and run her race to the end. The last phase of her life and the most strikingly effective one had begun with that searing statement of Gandhi which had sent her off to India to make her own response. That leaves those of us who are familiar with the life of Olive Allerton with the regret that it is no longer possible to put to Gandhi the question:

"What do you think of Christianity *now*?"

Epilogue

Olive's life is over but her influence lives on. Her work at "Beatitudes" and MITHRA made its mark on some of the staff and students of Rostrevor College – a school conducted by the Christian Brothers in Adelaide. Through the contact Olive had with the college, Brother Rob Callen was put in touch with Sister Theodore at MITHRA, and a visit to India was arranged for the Christmas holiday of 1988/89. For twelve months the school community raised funds so that the nine students and three staff who visited MITHRA, spending ten days working with the handicapped children, were able to take $16,000 for distribution to MITHRA, Mother Teresa and the Christian Brothers in Calcutta.

In the twelve months since their return this group has made a great impact on the school community of Rostrevor, on numerous schools and groups where they have presented the audio-visual kit recording their trip, on Adelaide television and on national television through the programme *Sixty Minutes*.

The ripples caused by Olive's life keep spreading out!

Acknowledgements

The story told in this book is based on Olive's recollection of her life as related to me in her last years at Lewis Nursing Home in Norwood, South Australia. Subsequently I verified the facts as far as possible through visits to India, Kenya and to England while travelling from Australia to the UK on other business. However, I was unable to research several facets of Olive's early life and corroborate personally what she told me.

This is therefore essentially Olive's story as told by Olive herself – she read the first draft and made some significant corrections. Towards the end of the twelve months during which I was piecing together her saga, her brain tumour became more acute and there were times when she was confused – details from one incident would be jumbled up with those from another time and place. However, Jean and Bill have checked the story – to them and their spouses Michael and Gill my sincerest thanks.

I wish to express my appreciation to a host of people who have assisted in a variety of ways: Brother Gerry Faulkner for making publication possible, Brothers Kevin McMaster, Terry Hann and John Baldwin of Rostrevor College, Father Adrian van Kaam, the Anglican parish priest of Seacliff Park, the Rev. Tom Jones and his wife Judy for use of their house at Goolwa on two writing stints and for typing the manuscript, Miss Sandy Mitchell, Mrs Dafne Jones and Brother Aidan Doherty for constructive criticism of the text.

In Africa I am indebted to Sister Marie Heintz and the

Missionary Sisters of Our Lady of Africa for guidance and transport around Kenya, at Kitale, Sep and Helen Mayer, Father Tom Smith and Brother Mike Hegarty; in Nairobi, Alan Knight and Molly Ryan, Father Eddie Woo and the White Fathers; the Holy Ghost Fathers in Mombasa, Father Cerezolli and the Verona Fathers at Tartar; Brother Ignatius Chincotta and my confrères in Gbarnga, Liberia.

In India the Salesian Fathers at Beatitudes, especially Fathers Tarcisius Ratnaswamy and Ittyachen Manjil, and at St Mary's Co-Cathedral Father Paul Kp and Community. Father Bede Griffiths and Sister Marie Louise Cuthina of Shantivanam and Ananda Ashrams, Lionel and Marlene Camoens of Madras, Sisters Theodore and Patricia at MITHRA, Brothers Bill Harrison and Jerome Kelly of the Christian Brothers in Calcutta, Brothers Das and Abraham of the Missionaries of Charity in Kiddepore (Calcutta), and Father Christie Daniel of Quilon.

In England Bishop Murphy O'Connor and Fathers David Sutcliff and Tony Shelley of Larundel/Brighton diocese and Worthing, Mrs Longley and staff at Roedean, Sam Fripp, Victor and Christine Mossor, Toby and Dorothy Rance. Brothers Liguori Gillespie and Dominic Sassi and the Brothers' Community at St Edward's College, Liverpool, who hosted me while the first part of the book was being written and who have provided me with a home from home. Brother Augustine Anthony has acted as liaison for me while I have been working in West Africa, and Teresa de Bertodano of Collins Fount has enabled seemingly insurmountable obstacles to be overcome.

To these and all others who have helped, my prayerful thanks.

Christian Brothers' Novitiate Community, Gbarnga, Liberia.
Feast of Pentecost 1990